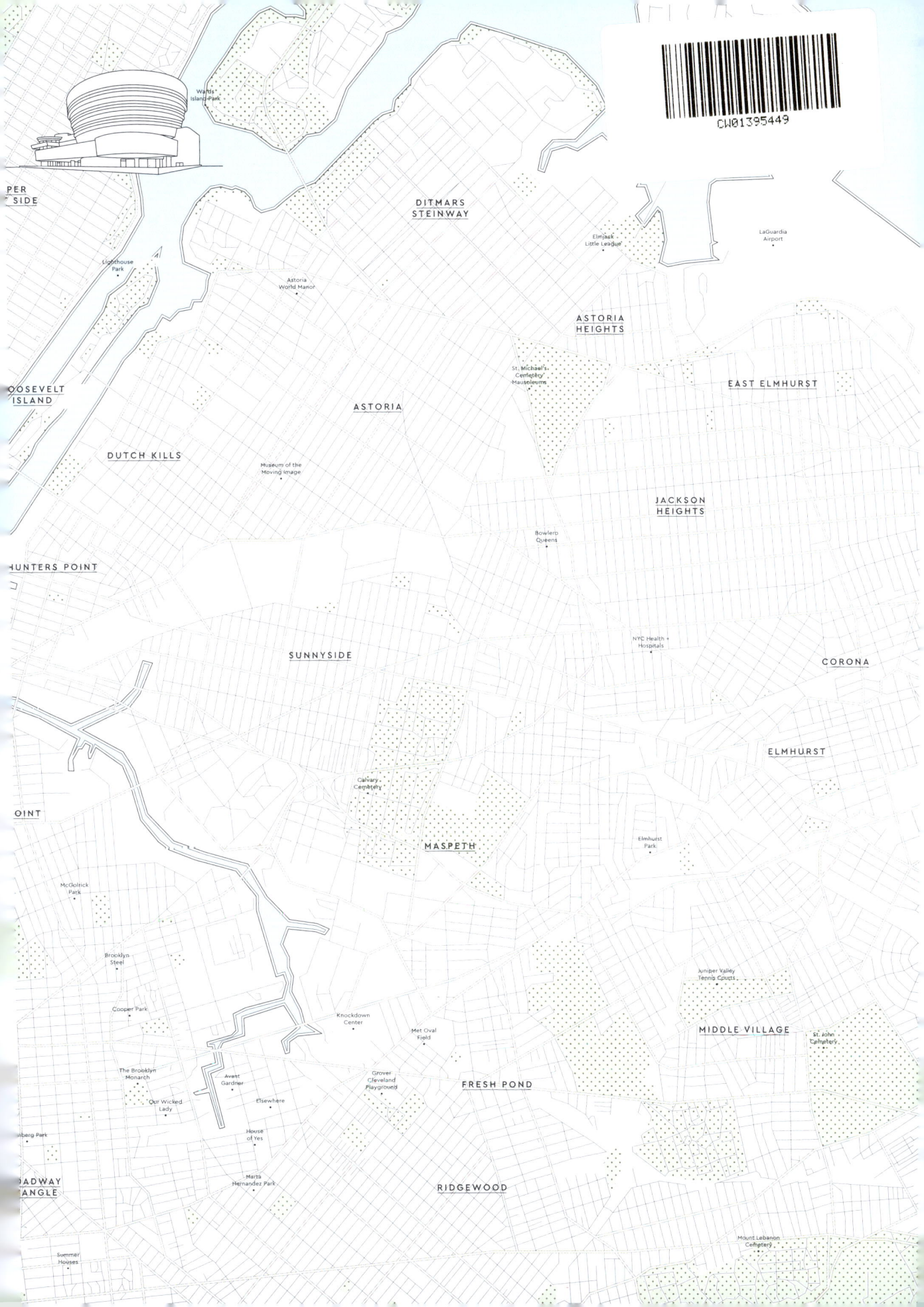

PER SIDE

DITMARS STEINWAY

Elmjack Little League

LaGuardia Airport

ASTORIA HEIGHTS

Lighthouse Park

Astoria World Manor

EAST ELMHURST

St. Michael's Cemetery Mausoleums

ROOSEVELT ISLAND

ASTORIA

DUTCH KILLS

Museum of the Moving Image

JACKSON HEIGHTS

Bowlero Queens

HUNTERS POINT

SUNNYSIDE

NYC Health + Hospitals

CORONA

ELMHURST

Calvary Cemetery

POINT

MASPETH

Elmhurst Park

McGolrick Park

Juniper Valley Tennis Courts

Brooklyn Steel

MIDDLE VILLAGE

St. John Cemetery

Cooper Park

Knockdown Center

Met Oval Field

The Brooklyn Monarch

Avant Gardner

Grover Cleveland Playground

FRESH POND

Our Wicked Lady

Elsewhere

berg Park

House of Yes

BROADWAY TRIANGLE

Marta Hernandez Park

RIDGEWOOD

Summer Houses

Mount Lebanon Cemetery

NEW YORK CITY

THE EXTRAORDINARY GUIDES

NEW YORK

MURIEL FRANÇOISE | SYLVIE LI

Rizzoli UNIVERSE

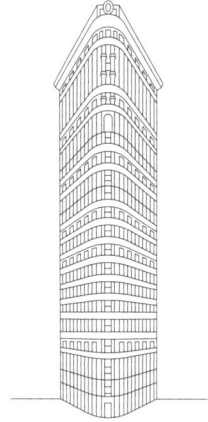

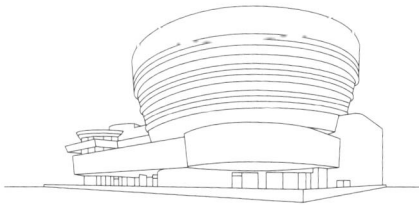

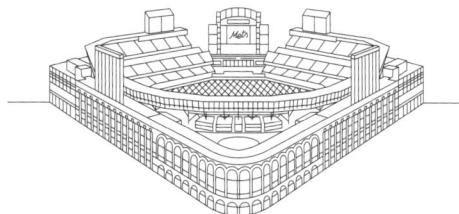

INTRODUCTION

New York City inspires an entire gallery of images. Lives glimpsed through Edward Hopper's windows, Georgia O'Keeffe's skyscrapers sparkling against the night sky, Patti Smith and Robert Mapplethorpe's bohemian existence in the Chelsea Hotel, Marilyn Monroe's flirtatious innocence over that subway vent, Audrey Hepburn's nonchalant elegance in front of the Tiffany's display window, Saul Leiter's rainy streets: the city has long fascinated people, inspiring and nurturing the most deep-seated of dreams.

It's difficult to imagine the landscape of Manhattan as Lenape territory before its conquest by Europeans in the 16th century, which ultimately led to the creation of New York. Its hills, forests, rivers, ponds, and beaches with distant sightings of whales, were enough for the natives to subsist, but trade and successive waves of migration would shape these watery stretches of land into today's metropolis with its teeming population of latter-day nomads.

The city that has given its name to the state within which it stands has more than eight million inhabitants and covers an area of just over 300 square miles (785 km²). It comprises five boroughs (Manhattan, Brooklyn, the Bronx, Queens, and Staten Island), each with its own identity developed over the years and through the endeavors of generations of residents, often with foreign roots. There are so many places for visitors to explore, eyes and ears wide open, and the first-time traveler will be surprised to note that the forest of skyscrapers in Manhattan is only a tiny part of a city made up of neighborhoods in which the natural world is never far away, whether it is the gigantic green lung of Central Park, the Atlantic shore, community gardens sandwiched between apartment blocks, or even farms perched on top of industrial buildings.

While New York is not America (as the news occasionally reminds us), it certainly offers an undeniable foretaste of the country. It is a place of profound and sometimes troubling contrasts, and leaves its mark on all those who come to visit. A stay in New York charges you with new energy as the city is in constant flux, like the landscape itself, repeatedly and boldly reinventing itself. This book will take you down roads less traveled and, most importantly, introduce you to New Yorkers from every walk of life, all of whom are fired by a remarkable community spirit.

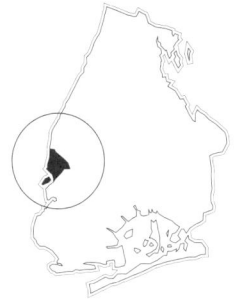

LOWER MANHATTAN

Most of the great symbols of New York huddle together at the southernmost end of Manhattan Island, the cradle of the city. The devastated area that once housed the twin towers of the World Trade Center continues its rebirth with admirable resilience, while the Lower East Side and Chinatown maintain traditions derived from immigration surrounded by new galleries and stores with carefully curated displays.

P . 8

*Choose from the many small restaurants in Chinatown
to sample some tasty cooking.*

OPPOSITE

*The Oculus, designed by the Spanish architect Santiago Calatrava above
the World Trade Center PATH station, looks like a modern cathedral.*

Squeezed between the Hudson and the East River, the southern tip of Manhattan Island is a stunning embodiment of the American dream, and its towering skyscrapers stand as modern temples to the glory of the United States' flagship city. It is difficult to picture the swampy ground that met the first Dutch colonists when they arrived to establish a trading post to barter with the Algonquin Indians in the 17th century. These pioneers of the New World had to negotiate a terrain of uneven banks and shores as they somehow tried to establish a city, and the twists and turns of the thoroughfares they laid down remain one of the distinctive features of this corner of Manhattan to this day.

A few of the streets tucked away at the very foot of the office blocks are reminders of the original founding of the city, and the old and the contemporary often intermingle. The churches, monuments, and buildings constructed by the settlers form a striking contrast to the towers of the Financial District. The New York Stock Exchange has stood here since 1817, its rollercoaster rides watched breathlessly by the entire world. Impeccably dressed individuals hurry along in the shadow of gigantic buildings, and amid a maze of streets stands the imposing presence of One World Trade Center, freighted with history, with its 104 floors and a height of 1,776 feet (541 m). The tower erected on Ground Zero, the site destroyed during the attacks of September 11, 2001, is the beating heart of an area enjoying a remarkable renaissance.

The Lower East Side is a fair walk from here, but will transport you into a far more rough-and-ready environment shaped by generations of immigrants since the turn of the 19th century. As in the neighboring district of Chinatown, you will find brick buildings housing tiny, old-fashioned businesses, including the Jewish deli of Russ & Daughters on East Houston Street, a must-visit if you fancy one of the best bagels in town. The restaurants, art galleries, boutiques, and interiors shops that have opened since the 2010s have attracted a somewhat younger crowd that has followed in the footsteps of many designers and artists in happily settling in neighborhoods where the rents are more affordable than elsewhere.

While the scenery of lower Manhattan need not detain you longer than necessary, the waterfront and Battery Park are good places to unwind in between more educational forays. To enjoy a spot of nature, head to the former military outpost of Governors Island, a few minutes away by ferry in high season; with its Neoclassical and Federal-style homes, fort, gardens, hiking trails, and vast lawns, it is a great vantage point from which to admire the Lower Manhattan skyline.

THE ESSENTIALS

01

ONE WORLD TRADE CENTER

This 1,776-ft (541-m) glass tower designed by American architect David Childs
stands on Ground Zero, the site of the Twin Towers destroyed during the attacks
of September 11, 2001. The tallest building in the city opened in 2014.

02

CHINATOWN

One of the largest Chinese communities outside Asia lives in this neighborhood.

03

SPRUCE STREET

This residential tower block rising above the Financial District, has 76 floors. The building has a sculpted steel facade that is the work of Canadian architect Frank Gehry.

04

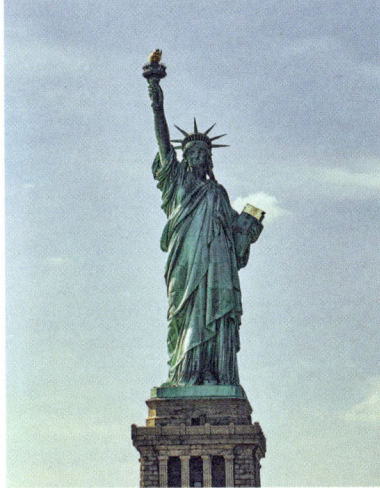

LIBERTY ISLAND

Liberty Island and the famous Statue of Liberty designed by Frédéric Auguste Bartholdi are only a short ferry ride away.

05

BATTERY PARK

This park owes its name to the artillery batteries installed at the turn of the 19th century.

06

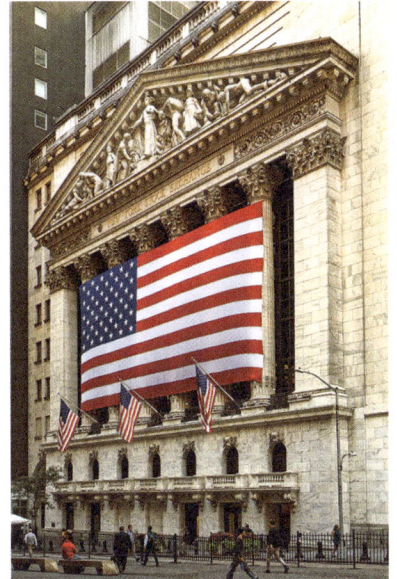

WALL STREET

Wall Street recalls the palisade that protected the Dutch from the Amerindians in the 17th century. The facade of the New York Stock Exchange, constructed in 1903, borrows features from Roman temples.

07

ELLIS ISLAND

This island was the entrance to the United States from 1892 until 1954, and now houses the Ellis Island National Museum of Immigration.

ABOVE

Enjoy a ferry ride to Liberty Island and Ellis Island from Battery Park.

OPPOSITE

*Waiting for the last boat to Manhattan on the Ellis Island
quayside on a summer evening.*

PORTRAIT

THE ULTIMATE HOSTESS

Designer Sophie Lou Jacobsen's daily life is full of imagination. From her
Lower East Side loft, she dreams up objects made of glass and metal that
elevate the most banal activities into joyful daily rituals.

A tiny green vase mounted on a pink pedestal like a trophy, a throne for an egg or perhaps some toothpicks, or a goblet that opens up like a delicate flower for Champagne or a sorbet: such items may seem perfectly ordinary at first, but through their very presence on a table, they embody a certain art of living. The designer Sophie Lou Jacobsen has cultivated a taste for setting the stage for daily life, an exercise in style that she enjoys practicing in her loft on the Lower East Side, situated in an old school. "I have the good fortune to be accompanied by objects I have designed, to be able to arrange them in constantly different ways, and to continue my artistic explorations through them," she observes, surrounded by objects that are as unique as her own creative approach.

After a couple of years in the Red Hook neighborhood followed by a stop in Gowanus, Brooklyn, the designer elected to establish her apartment and studio in Lower Manhattan. "I wanted to live in the city, right in the middle of the energy it radiates, but also to be able to receive visitors in my own space more easily, especially for afternoon drinks." With parents originating from Denmark and Poland and a nomadic childhood that took her from Seattle to Paris, Sophie learned to appreciate the cultural richness of the world at an early age. She has been living in New York since 2015, after studying design in London. It was while taking part in an exhibition by the Furnishing Utopia collective,

who reinterpret the legacy of the Shakers (followers of a religious movement now considered the founders of American design in the 18th century) that she realized and mastered the unsuspected qualities of glass, and she then learned how to tame the medium with the help of local artisan glassmakers.

She strives constantly to forge links between humans and the objects that surround them. "My creations evolve around simple activities like eating, drinking, receiving guests, or decorating a room with flowers. I take pains to create surprising moments to encourage people toward a greater enjoyment of life's little pleasures." For Sophie, objects stand out in design terms through their bold lines and colors, and her studio features lamps created in collaboration with the New York brand In Common With and opalescent and amber glass vases inspired by Art Nouveau.

Since settling in Manhattan, she has been taking lots of walks and discovering places steeped in history, like the bars that feed her imagination. "In my work, I love to subvert traditional expectations like with the contours of a glass, for example, to which I add undulations." The beauty of her objects is also in their versatility, which is all the more welcome in the small spaces of large cities. "You can put flowers in a carafe, pencils in a cup, and a dessert in a cocktail glass", Sophie adds.

CURIOSITIES

The designer's imaginative and elegant
creations in glass and metal adorn an interior
bathed in light.

A LITANY OF DELIGHTS

Ensconced in her Lower East Side loft, the designer
Sophie Lou Jacobsen cultivates a lifestyle that is
nurtured by her French roots.

ABOVE

*The Staten Island ferry offers free views of the Statue of Liberty
and the Lower Manhattan skyline.*

OPPOSITE

*The old military outpost of Governors Island offers visitors a pleasant
green space and is only a short ferry ride away.*

SKYSCRAPERS

The imposing edifices that rose up across the landscape of
Manhattan at the dawn of the 19th century paved the way for ever
taller skyscrapers, and now the city's horizon, punctuated by
tower blocks, has become iconic.

The towers reaching for the New York sky were not a local invention but instead the apotheosis of an idea imported from Chicago. The Illinois metropolis had seen them as a quick way of securing housing with a minimal footprint on the ground, and the first skyscraper appeared in 1884, thanks to the architect Louis H. Sullivan. New York, which was faced with a huge influx of immigrants, then set about a series of increasingly ambitious architectural projects at the southern end of Manhattan, where the ground was sufficiently solid.

These architectural feats were possible only thanks to the Elisha Otis invention of a safety brake for elevators in 1853 and the metal-framed structures that were much lighter than brickwork. The Flatiron, with its 21 floors and tapering facade, was one of the city's first skyscrapers. The businessmen running the show were always aiming higher, however, and the Woolworth Building, completed in 1913, would go on to hold the title of world's tallest building for seventeen years. The 1930s saw a movement toward monumental projects, including the Chrysler Building (77 floors) and the Empire State Building (102 floors). The twin towers of the World Trade Center (110 floors), built in the 1970s, were to look out over the surrounding skyscrapers of Lower Manhattan for nearly thirty years.

As fashion and technology have moved on, skyscrapers have been equipped with all kinds of ornamentation and have sometimes taken on highly idiosyncratic dimensions. The city is increasingly being used as an outlet for expression by master architects from America and overseas, encouraged by daring entrepreneurs. The 2010s saw the advent of extremely slender buildings, the so-called pencil towers, such as the residential projects at 432 Park Avenue (85 floors) and 111 West 57th Street, aka the Steinway Tower (84 floors) in Midtown. The adapted structure of the latter's tip (1,427 feet/435 m in the air) can sway up to three feet (a meter), allowing it to resist the force of the wind. Permission to soar so high into the sky required the developers of such towers to buy up the unused "air rights" of the adjacent buildings.

Environmental considerations are now a priority for the architects and engineers behind the construction sites that are constantly springing up. Much as in the glory days of Art Deco, artists are often invited to contribute their talents, so try to linger (if you are allowed) in the entrance of a building to admire this mosaic or that botanical installation, or even a carved bench. You will spot so many artistic touches, free to all to enjoy.

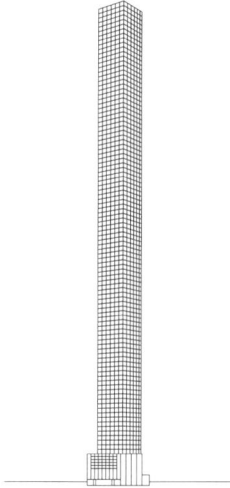

432 PARK AVENUE

Height: 1,396 feet/426 m
Year: 2016 **Floors:** 85

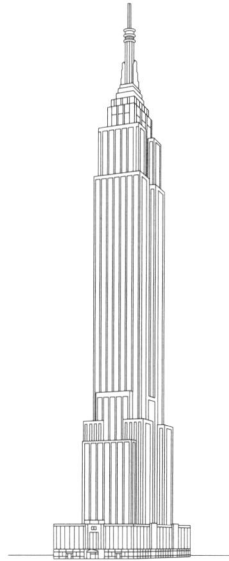

EMPIRE STATE BUILDING

Height: 1.454 feet/443 m
Year: 1931 **Floors:** 102

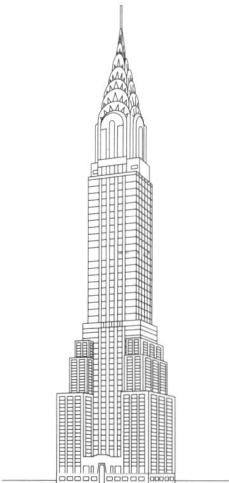

CHRYSLER BUILDING

Height: 1.046 feet/319 m
Year: 1930 **Floors:** 77

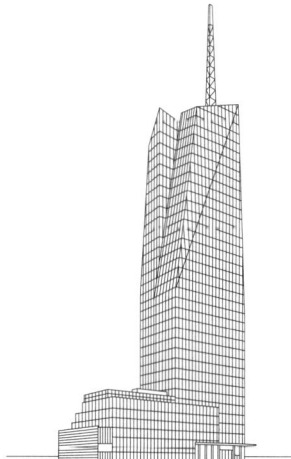

BANK OF AMERICA TOWER

Height: 944.5 feet/288 m
Year: 2009 **Floors:** 55

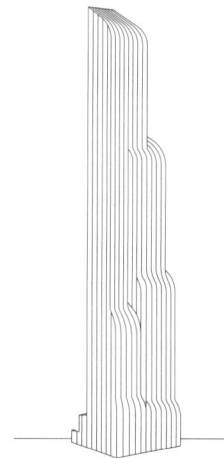

ONE57

Height; 1,005 feet/306 m
Year: 2013 **Floors:** 75

VERTICAL DEVELOPMENT

Wealthy New Yorkers, real estate companies, and local developers were seized by
a desire for elevation from the end of the 19th century. Steel allowed them to dream
of increasingly high towers and glass gave them views over the whole world.

ABOVE

The sculpture Group of Four Trees *was created by the artist French Jean Dubuffet
for the headquarters of the Chase Manhattan Bank in the Financial District.*

OPPOSITE

Completed in 1931, the limestone facade of One Wall Street has Art Deco lines.

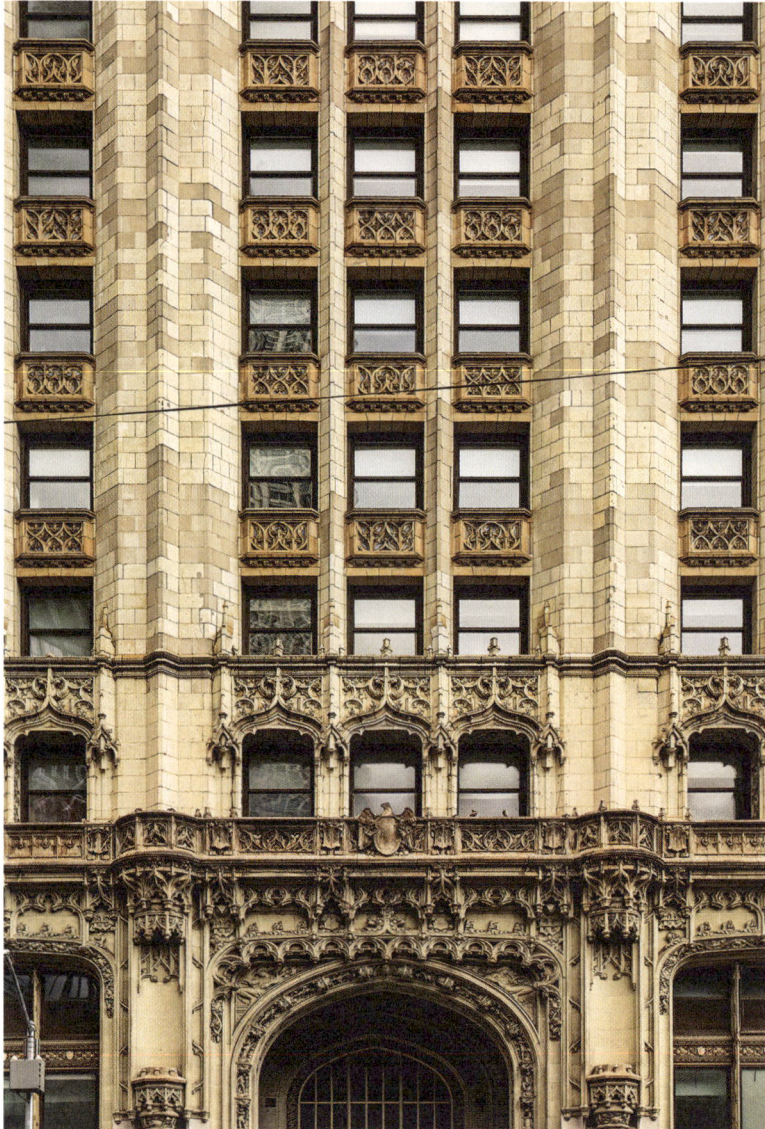

ABOVE

The Gothic Revival-style Woolworth Building held the record as the world's tallest skyscraper from 1913 until 1930.

OPPOSITE

Trinity Church honors traditions inherited from the past amid the bustle of the Financial District.

EXCURSION

DESERT VINTAGE
PERIOD COSTUMES

Salima Boufelfel and Roberto Cowan upcycle elegant vintage ladies' and gents' clothes in a discreet boutique on the Lower East Side, with designs from the world's greatest couturiers.

You would be forgiven for walking past the Desert Vintage display window at 34 Orchard Street without giving it a second glance. You have to venture inside the former sporting goods store to fully appreciate the beauty, originality, and quality of the clothes, all meticulously preserved, just out of sight. This little-known outlet sells clothes from major fashion houses from the turn of the last century to the 1990s, all in perfect condition thanks to a rigorous selection procedure and the attentions of an expert seamstress. Yves Saint Laurent, Alaïa, Prada, Comme des Garçons, Chanel, Issey Miyake, and Balenciaga are just some of the names, along with a few forgotten labels from the 1920s that sold delicate dresses for the slender frames of the time.

New life is breathed into these rare pieces by Salima Boufelfel and Roberto Cowan, who have also owned a store in Tucson, Arizona, since 2012. Salima's interest in old clothes goes back to her high school years, when she took on the task of making theater costumes with the help of vintage stores that lent her clothes. Roberto, who was given a sewing machine for his thirteenth birthday, was also an early starter. When the owner of the Desert Vintage retro clothes store (where Salima was a regular customer) was thinking about closing down the business, the young couple took up the baton, and daringly mix and match eras in the ensembles they put together. Their experiments produced complete looks rather than dated styles.

Over time, the partners made friends with Emily Bode, who was ordering rare pieces from them, and acting on the advice offered by this pioneer of creating fashion from vintage fabrics and by her partner, Aaron Aujla, they decided to open a store near her outlet in Chinatown. Aaron worked with Green River Project, his architecture and interior design company, to create decors inspired by the Chelsea studio of the artist Louise Bourgeois. At his behest, the ceiling was removed, the walls stripped to a raw finish, family souvenirs were hung from a mirror, and an old bathtub was installed to increase the intimate feel of the store.

Since opening in 2022, Desert Vintage has attracted a very varied clientele: couples in love planning their wedding, stylists for an evening event, costume designers for a television series, or couturiers keen to explore the expertise of the previous generation. Salima works behind the scenes to design dresses for Ténéré, her own label, and these gauzy, elegant creations conjure up images of some sublime distant location, the landscapes of the desert from which she comes.

1/ BACKDROP

The decor in Salima Boufelfel and Roberto Cowan's boutique was inspired
by the artist Louise Bourgeois' studio in Chelsea.

2/ A SIGN

The boutique was formerly
a sportswear store.

3/ BATHTUB

An old bath emphasizes the
intimate nature of the place.

4/ MIX AND MATCH

The vintage clothes from major fashion
houses are arranged by color.

With the sun and sky reflecting in the glass facade that covers the 1,776-ft (541-m) skyscraper, One World Trade Center is an impressive sight from the water.

ABOVE

*Open-air stalls, signs written in Chinese, and an authentic atmosphere
make Chinatown an exciting area to explore.*

OPPOSITE

*Kiki's restaurant at 130, Division Street, still has a Chinese sign on its
facade even though the menu is made up of exclusively Greek dishes.*

RUSS & DAUGHTERS

APPETIZERS

TRADITIONS

This narrow store at 179, E Houston Street on the Lower East Side
sells Jewish delicacies that would gladden the heart of Joel Russ,
who came over from Poland in 1904.

CAVIAR

The store sells an enormous variety of different caviars.

CHALLAH

These brioche-style loaves are shared with guests during Shabbat.

VARIETY

Russ & Daughters' selection of bagels includes a dark rye option.

FINESSE

It is a house rule that the smoked salmon must be cut very thinly by hand.

À LA CARTE

The bagels are worth the wait (which can sometimes be long).

VINTAGE

The store has changed very little since opening in 1920.

SMOKED FISH

There are eight kinds of smoked salmon for sale at Russ & Daughters.

CATERING

Many New Yorkers head here for high-quality weekend brunch ingredients.

ABOVE

Katz's Deli at 205, E Houston Street, is one of the most popular places recommended for meat-lovers on the Lower East Side.

OPPOSITE

Metal fire escapes began to be fixed to the facades of the tenements of the Lower East Side from 1867.

An old bronze clock still hangs from the facade of the old offices of the New York Sun *newspaper at 280, Broadway.*

With its Beaux-Arts-style facade, the Surrogate's Courthouse is one of the most beautiful buildings in the Civic Center.

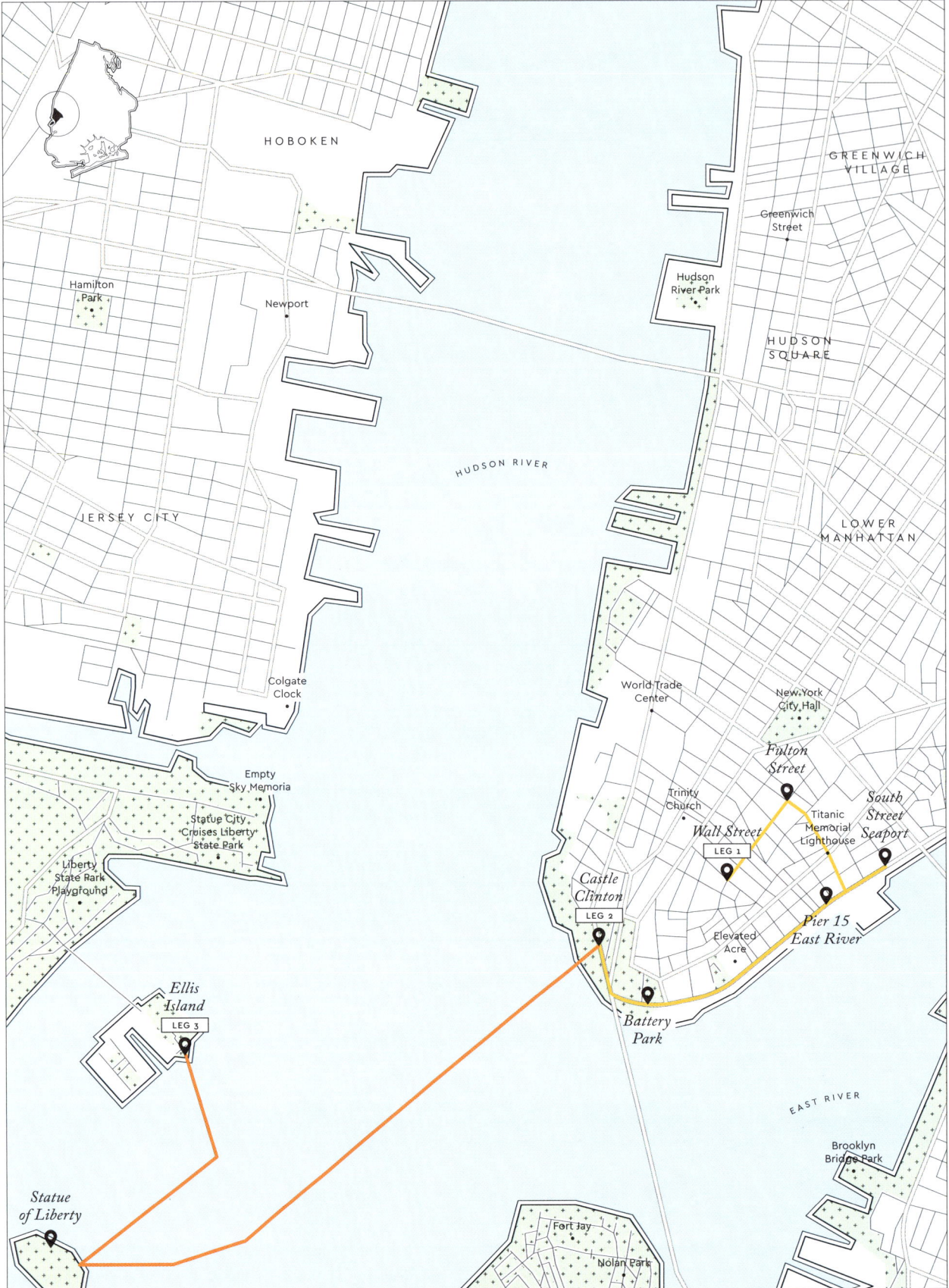

IN THE FOOTSTEPS OF PIONEERS

The southern tip of Manhattan Island is steeped in history and still bears the mark of the men and women who came here from Europe in the hope of a better life. Nestling at the bases of the skyscrapers of the Financial District, some places still offer albeit faint clues to lives of the past.

LEG 1 : SOUTH STREET SEAPORT

To get an idea of the impression their adopted land left on the first New Yorkers, you must be near the East River. Leaving Wall Street, head down Fulton Street and linger for a moment beside the Schermerhorn Row Block, an urban island of the oldest buildings in the city. The first floor of these former warehouses dating from 1811 now house small businesses that include McNally Jackson Books, a charming independent bookstore. Don't forget to call into the Titanic Memorial Lighthouse on the corner of Water Street and Fulton Street in the South Street Seaport; the beacon honors the passengers and crew of the famous liner that would have made landfall in New York on April 17, 1912, had it not hit an iceberg en route.

LEG 2 : CASTLE CLINTON

At the end of Fulton Street, take the passage beneath the South Street Viaduct and follow the waterside (with a brief stop at Pier 15) to Battery Park. This very pleasant green area, which includes gardens and a city farm, was developed on land reclaimed from the sea in the 19th century. At its southern end stands Castle Clinton, a circular fort built on an island between 1808 and 1811 to protect the artillery of the city's defenders from British attack. It was then converted into a restaurant and a venue for opera and theater productions. The arrival of large swathes of immigrants during the second half of the 19th century prompted the authorities to turn the building into a processing center, and it served this purpose until the job was given to Ellis Island in 1890. It was then used as an aquarium before closing its doors in 1941. It was designated a national monument in 1975 and is now the ticket office for Liberty Island and Ellis Island.

LEG 3 : ELLIS ISLAND

Head to the jetty opposite Castle Clinton and take a boat to Liberty Island (where the Statue of Liberty proudly stands) and Ellis Island. Before you return to Manhattan, enter the Beaux-Arts style building and explore the museum as you immerse yourself in the challenging adventure that was immigration at the turn of the 20th century. Between 1892 and 1954, upwards of 12 million people were stringently questioned and examined in this imposing building that looks more like a railroad station before being granted entry in order to seek their fortunes in the United States. The complex, which replaced wooden huts hastily erected on a former execution site for criminals, included a hospital for the isolation of the sick. The baggage depository, the enormous inspection hall, the dormitories, and the immigrants' photos and personal effects are particularly moving and shine a spotlight on the role played by these men and women who came from elsewhere to play a key role in the development of the nation.

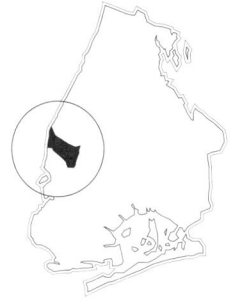

ARTY NEW YORK

Nestling between the Financial District and Midtown, the neighborhoods of TriBeCa, SoHo, the East Village, NoHo, Little Italy, Nolita, the Bowery, Greenwich Village, and Chelsea form an astonishing urban patchwork. Their fashion boutiques and art and design galleries lure local shoppers, while artists create new works in lofts away from prying eyes as they revive the bohemian spirit of the New York of old.

The tragedy of September 11, 2001 at the World Trade Center dealt the adjacent neighborhood of TriBeCa a severe blow. Laid out in a vague triangle between Canal Street and Chinatown, the area is now experiencing a stunning renaissance thanks in particular to several players on the artistic scene, and increasing numbers of galleries have chosen to open in the neighboring streets of SoHo. This is a slightly quieter area for a stroll and can sometimes seem a little rough-and-ready as you thread your way between old warehouses and the homes of wealthy families. Artists, designers, and gallery owners even throw open the doors or their apartments, either by appointment or during exhibitions, offering a more human aspect to the creative process and allowing their community to show their work outside the usual forums.

Around the corner, the display windows of SoHo compete to entice passers-by into the interiors of outlets for local or international labels. All that remains of the 1960s, a period in which artists took over the lofts left empty by businesses, is the former apartment and studio of Donald Judd at 101 Spring Street, which is open to the public by appointment. The terraces of buildings with their cast-iron facades are worth a visit, however. The galleries here also display the avant-garde of contemporary design in old workshops, and emerging designers have been invited to personalize the interiors of stores and restaurants.

Greenwich Village was founded by the British in 1696 and has been a haunt of writers, creative types, and rebels of every kind since the 19th century, when docks were built along the Hudson, causing the local middle classes to relocate. Simply follow your nose down its small streets lined with red-brick houses, keeping an eye out for gardens behind railings, and, before returning, pause for a moment in a café and imagine Edward Hopper painting at a window overlooking Washington Square. Political demonstrations are often held in this park, which is laid out around a Beaux-Arts-style triumphal arch, and with the campus of New York University (NYU) just round the corner, the area buzzes with imagination and ideas.

Chelsea is the last bastion of cool before the excesses of Midtown and is a mix of extraordinary eclecticism. The quiet streets of its historic heart lead to the High Line, an old elevated railroad track that was converted into a green promenade at the turn of the 2000s. The area's once bohemian spirit has been somewhat diluted by the ambitious projects that followed, but you might try to find traces at the Chelsea Hotel, whose former residents include Patti Smith, Robert Mapplethorpe, and Leonard Cohen. This legendary establishment is still home to several artists who have resisted Manhattan housing pressure and now have their homes amongst the tourists and photographers in search of iconic snaps.

THE ESSENTIALS

08

THE *VESSEL*

The futuristic architecture of the *Vessel*, designed by Thomas Heatherwick,
is one of the main attractions in the new neighborhood of Hudson Yards.

09

HISTORIC GREENWICH VILLAGE

The oldest part of Greenwich Village was classified as one of the city's Historic Districts in 1969.

10

WASHINGTON SQUARE

A marble triumphal arch by architect Stanford White was unveiled in 1895, replacing a wooden arch erected six years previously to mark the centenary of George Washington's accession to the presidency of the United States.

11

NEW MUSEUM

This museum in the Bowery is the work of Japanese architects Kazuyo Seijima and Ryue Nishizawa.

12

CHELSEA MARKET

A popular destination for foodies, the market has found a home on the first floor of an old biscuit factory next to the High Line.

13

GREENWICH VILLAGE

There are still signs of the bohemian spirit of the artists who once lived in the Village, especially in the Jefferson Market Courthouse, built in 1877, which is now a library building.

14

WITHNEY MUSEUM

The Whitney Museum of American Art has more than 3 000 paintings by Edward Hopper, and there are spectacular views across the city, the High Line, and Little Island from its terraces.

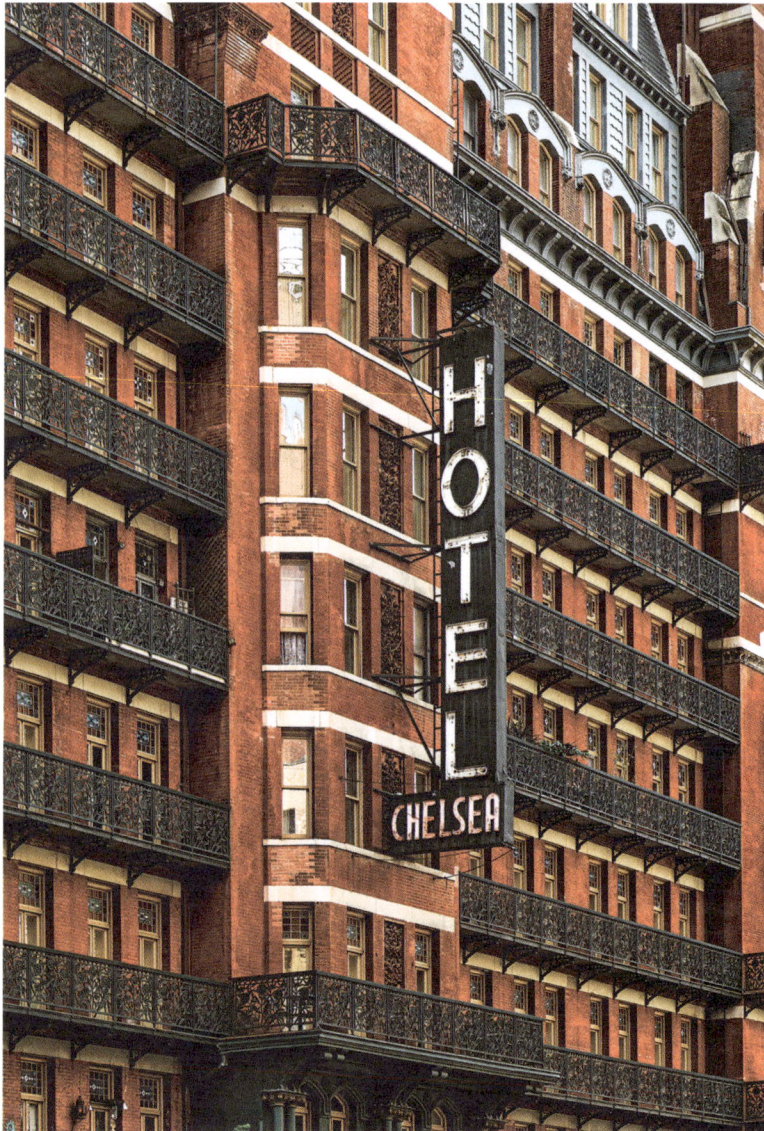

ABOVE

*The Chelsea Hotel was once a haunt of artists on New York's underground scene
and one of the city's first private housing co-ops.*

OPPOSITE

*Nature and concrete coexist in Chelsea,
as on so many Manhattan streets.*

Visitors to the Le Bain bar on the roof of the Standard Hotel
can enjoy a panoramic view over Lower Manhattan.

ABOVE

From the High Line, you have a particularly good view
of 520 West 28th, the work of architect Zaha Hadid.

OPPOSITE

The parkland of Little Island was created by sinking concrete pillars in the
Hudson to be used as giant pots for luxuriant and varied vegetation.

ARCHITECTURE

CAST-IRON BUILDINGS IN SOHO

450 BROOME STREET

The 1850s saw the use of prefabricated parts and machine-made molds
to blend steel and stone for buildings in SoHo.

561-563 BROADWAY

The manufacturer of Singer sewing machines commissioned architect Ernest Flagg to design the Little Singer Building.

109 PRINCE STREET

J. Morgan Slade reinterpreted Renaissance French style for this building in the old Silk District.

469-475 BROOME STREET

The Gunther Building was built in 1871–2 and needed curved windows to match the angle at its corner.

451 BROOME STREET

The architectural exuberance of the Silk Exchange Building has earned it the nickname of the Wedding Cake.

435 BROOME STREET

The Victorian Gothic Revival style selected for this facade demonstrates the sophistication of this innovative construction technique in the 19th century.

575 BROADWAY

This 1882 building on the corner of Broadway and Prince Street now houses an annex of the Guggenheim Museum.

SOPHISTICATION

The architects took pleasure in conjuring up the past with many decorative details.

IN COLOR

To complement their industrial elegance, cast-iron buildings could be painted different colors.

ABOVE

*The awnings over residential building entrances are integral
parts of the West Village landscape.*

OPPOSITE

*Lunch on a terrace is one of the pleasures of an afternoon spent
in the West Village and surrounding area.*

HISTORY

THE HIGH LINE
NATURE'S INDUSTRY

A park snakes its way 30 feet (9 m) above the streets of the Meatpacking District and Chelsea, following the route of a railroad track that once supplied the area with goods. Through the dedication of local residents, the formerly disused site is now home to gardens dotted with works of art.

Before construction of the High Line was completed between 20th Avenue and the Hudson River in 1929, the railroad traversed the daily to and fro of New Yorkers, with all the dangers that such proximity brought with it, hence 10th Avenue's nickname Death Avenue. The new track, opened in 1934, allowed trains to deliver goods (particularly milk, eggs, cheese, and meat from the region's farms) directly to the upper floors of the warehouses between Gansevoort Street and 34th Street.

The advent of the automobile and the construction of major road arteries resulted in the demolition of the southern stretch of the High Line and a slowdown in activity; the last consignment of turkeys was dropped off in 1980. Nature reclaimed the abandoned structure and though it was a sight for sore eyes for lovers of wild gardens, the area remained inaccessible to the public. An architect came up with the idea of transforming the track into a park and to convert the surrounding warehouses into lofts and social housing. Unfortunately, the mayor of New York in the 1990s preferred the demolition option.

The rest of the story is one of a popular revolt that will be forever part of High Line history. In 1999, the Friends of the High Line committee created by Joshua David and Robert Hammond, two local residents, set themselves the task of turning the railroad into an elevated green space and the walkway they suggested was inspired by Paris's *Coulée Verte*. Architects, designers, and gardeners helped to shape the garden, which was opened to the public in 2009 and is now maintained largely by volunteers. The development was carried out in several stages in accordance with public and private support. The High Line has provided access to the new Hudson Yards area since 2023.

Various kinds of garden alternate along the route, from the wildest to the most meticulously tended, punctuated by works of art supplied by the High Line Art project. The once-derelict surroundings have also undergone a remarkable transformation, and the futurist architecture of buildings that include projects by Frank Gehry, Jean Nouvel, and Zaha Hadid, stand out in a landscape that tended to be rather concrete-heavy in places. While it is certainly difficult to imagine a trip to New York without visiting the gardens that have risen from the city's industrial heritage, and coming here in high season will allow you to enjoy a colorful spectacle, it will often be in the middle of a dense crowd. The ideal time to visit is the fall, when the low, late-afternoon sunlight gets lost amongst the flowers and dreamers can enjoy the delicate dried branches, sometimes sprinkled in hoar frost.

Strollers in this elevated urban park can enjoy a panorama that includes views of the Empire State Building.

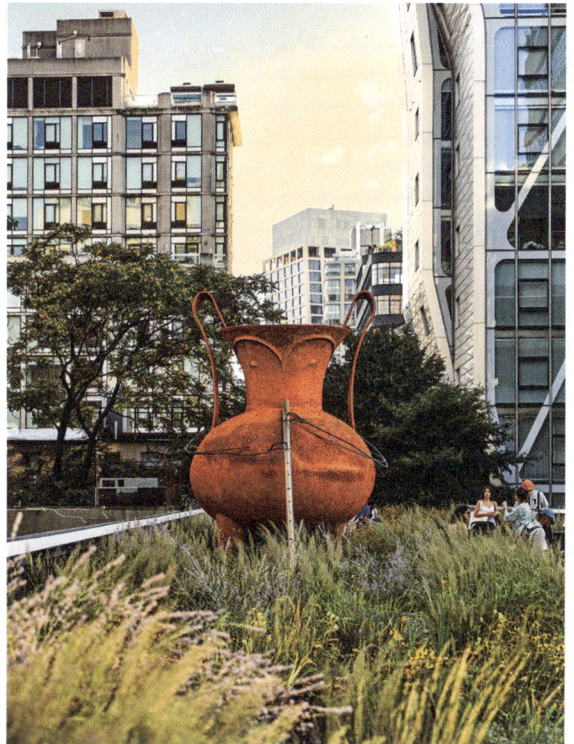

INSTALLATIONS

Public artworks created for the High Line adorn the route amongst the plants and flowers.

ABOVE

*Freemans restaurant and its classic menu of hearty dishes await at the end
of a graffiti-adorned alley on the Lower East Side.*

OPPOSITE

*XOCO 325 was built on the site of an old SoHo chocolate factory in 2016,
and took inspiration from local cast-iron buildings for its aluminum facade.*

LANDON METZ
A PAINTER OF THE EPHEMERAL

From his studio in an old TriBeCa factory, the Arizona-born painter
Landon Metz is perfecting an artistic language whose rhythms adorn his canvases
with abstract shapes shrouded in poetry.

As Manhattan was emerging from a long period of lethargy caused by the COVID-19 pandemic, Landon Metz left his studio in Bushwick, Brooklyn, to move into an old factory in TriBeCa at the invitation of his designer friend Giancarlo Valle, who had just set up an office there. His space is perched high over Chinatown, overlooking the busy street. The painter has created order in the calm of an immaculate workshop like a gigantic canvas, from which his works emerge, his paints meticulously stored in plastic bottles and strange containers. It is definitely a space that is conducive to creativity.

Hailing from Phoenix, Landon elected to put down roots in New York to develop his career within a vibrant and supportive artistic community. The years he spent in the desert shaped his imagination: "My childhood in Arizona left an indelible mark on my visual language and my perception of time and space. This dry environment taught me a great deal about economy of shapes and media", he emphasizes. His works are characterized by monochromatic shapes with organic contours that echo or respond to one another in a void incarnated by white. They bear the imprint of the ephemeral gestures and thoughts or states that accompany them.

To help with concentration, the painter has surrounded himself with furniture and small objects that match his own style, minimalist yet joyful. Many of these objects have been designed by Italian designers, in particular Gaetano Pesce and Ettore Sottsass, who founded the Memphis Group in 1980. The rituals that he carries out in these austere surroundings (such as preparing his watercolors and canvases or looking after his plants) help to induce the meditative state that is an essential part of his art.

The artist's canvases have been exhibited around the world from London to Seoul, taking in Copenhagen and Dubai. Marimekko, the famous Finnish company, was receptive to his poetic universe and invited him to design some patterns for a collection of clothes and accessories that was unveiled in 2023. Despite the many requests that come his way, when he is not painting, Landon keeps himself to himself in an old church in Brooklyn Heights, with his wife Hanna, a fashion designer, for company. Their son Èze is also a talented artist and some of his works, just as mysterious as his father's, are to be found in Landon's studio.

Painter Landon Metz's workshop
celebrates color and organic shapes
like a giant canvas.

SILENCE

Despite being located in the middle of a busy
neighborhood, a deep calm reigns throughout the
artist's creative universe.

In 2024, gallery-owner Amélie du Chalard opened a space dedicated to
collectors in an old artist's studio at 85–87, Mercer Street in SoHo.

There's something quite magical about the late afternoon light
falling on the buildings of SoHo.

URBAN CHALLENGES

SOLUTIONS AND INVENTIONS

Housing has posed technical problems for both architects and local authorities as the city has been built, and the safety and comfort of their fellow city dwellers has required them to find solutions that now form part of the urban landscape.

The iron fire escapes adorning the facades of New York buildings have become icons of the city, and their presence is connected with the great waves of immigration in the 19th century. These major influxes of people encouraged real estate developers to construct buildings of five to seven floors known as tenements, with rooms arranged in rows and often without any ventilation. A fire that cost a dozen or so lives forced the local authorities to make the installation of fire escapes compulsory in 1867, and building owners constructed them on the outside to avoid sacrificing rentable space. It has been compulsory to build fire escapes on the inside since 1968, but the old metal structures have been retained on prewar homes. While New Yorkers are not averse to grabbing some fresh air on them, they are dangerous to use, given their great age.

The metal window grilles on residential buildings in many neighborhoods of New York are not necessarily guarantees of protection against intruders. They are often a safety measure to prevent the children of New York from falling to their deaths and in 1976, the city introduced a regulation that required safety bars to be fitted to windows of apartments where children under ten lived. Only windows leading to a fire escape were allowed to be freely accessible.

There are still air-conditioning units on the facades of many buildings, even if they do not always work. The grilles installed on the windows are sometimes shaped to match these machines that revolutionized daily life for New Yorkers faced with hot and humid summers. The world has Willis Haviland Carrier to thank for the first modern air-conditioner prototype in 1902, which was constructed with the aim of improving air quality in a Brooklyn printer's. A/C units were initially the preserve of public and official spaces (and of the rich) before becoming universally available. Nowadays, they have often been replaced by HVAC systems built into homes or portable equipment that can be packed away during cooler months.

Visible from far across the New York horizon, the large wooden cisterns of the water towers installed on old buildings more than six stories high served a domestic purpose as a result of the need for sufficient water pressure. These tanks began to appear on the city's rooftops in the 19th century when homes began pointing skyward. They were filled by means of an electric pump, after which water was routed down pipes to the various floors using the force of gravity. The lifespan of a wooden cistern is about twenty-five years and installing them at these heights, using traditional techniques, requires a certain amount of calm and composure.

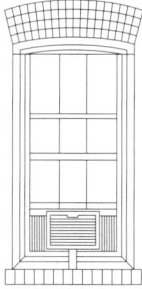

AIR-CONDITIONING UNIT

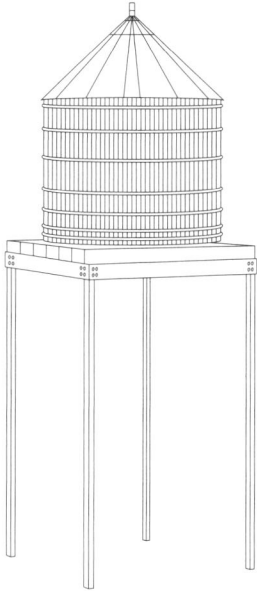

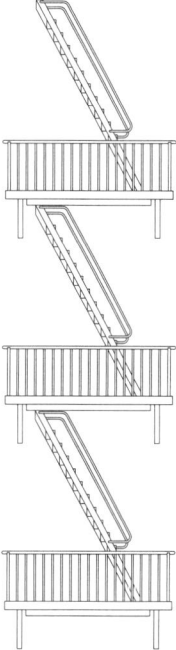

WATER TANK

FIRE ESCAPE

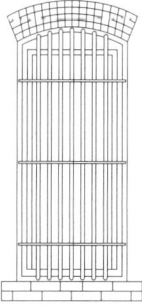

SAFETY GRILLE

URBAN PLANNING

Life in the hot and humid atmosphere of summer in vertical New York
has forced the city to find practical solutions for its residents.

ABOVE

*A small market selling local flowers and vegetables on a street corner
in TriBeCa.*

OPPOSITE

*With its steel columns and picture windows, the FORM Atelier gallery
bears witness to the enthusiasm for cast-iron architecture in TriBeCa.*

WEEHAWKEN

Days Point

HUDSON RIVER

Pier 88

Lorem ipsum

Riverside
Park South

UPPER
WEST SIDE

Lincoln Center
for the Performing Arts

Columbus
Circle

HELL'S
KITCHEN

Jacob Javits
Covention
Center

Music
Hall

Times
Square

Little
Brazil

Bryant
Park

The Vessel

LEG 3

The Edge

Madison
Square Garden

Empire
State Building

*High
Line*

LEG 2

Chelsea
Waterside

Castle Point

Pier 51

*Little
Island*

LEG 1

Standard
Hotel

*Chelsea
Market*

Flatiron
Building

*Whitney
Museum
of American Art*

Union
Square

GREENWICH
VILLAGE

Greenwich
Street

Washington
Square Park

Hudson River
Park Trust

A STROLL ALONG THE HUDSON

The Hudson River lying alongside Manhattan's western shores resembles a glittering ribbon when the sun's rays hit it. Come and experience the charm of life by the water on the paths and byways built in and around the neighborhood of Chelsea.

LEG 1 : LITTLE ISLAND

A strangely shaped concrete structure pokes up out of the water near the old Pier 54, where the 705 survivors of the sinking of the *Titanic* in 1912 disembarked. Little Island is a manmade islet perched on stilts. From a distance, the 132 elements that make it up look rather like a bouquet of flowers hence its nickname Tulip Island. This leafy space opened in 2021 as part of a development project for the Hudson River Park stretching from 59th Street to Battery Park at the southern end of Manhattan Island, and is the work of designer Thomas Heatherwick (who can also lay claim to the *Vessel*, another architectural curiosity in the new neighborhood of Hudson Yards) and landscape architect Signe Nielsen. Access to the undulating terrain of this skyborne park is via two walkways, and its pillars of heights between 16 and 60 feet (5–18 m) act as gigantic pots in which more than 400 species of vegetation grow. Their outline was inspired by the patterns that naturally form around the old pillars nearby when the surrounding water turns to ice. To get a better view of this gift to New Yorkers from billionaire Barry Diller and his wife, fashion designer Diane von Fürstenberg, head for the terrace on the eighth floor of the Whitney Museum of American Art or the rooftop bar of the Standard Hotel.

LEG 2 : HIGH LINE

After checking out a couple of art galleries in Chelsea and stopping off at Chelsea Market (held in an old biscuit factory at number 75, 9th Avenue), ascend the walkway on 16th Street to reach the High Line, a park following an old railroad track, where you will find a multitude of plants, flowers, and bushes (looked after by gardeners and volunteers) in amongst the rails installed in the 1930s. Concrete can be seen on all sides and the place is often thronged with walkers, but there is still an unobtrusive tranquility (in places). You may find neighbors meditating on the bleachers and benches, or urban sketchers capturing this fascinating juxtaposition of nature and city. The view over the Hudson River from this gigantic balcony is a good reason to slow down and take a breath. Other stopping points that come highly recommended include the Plinth, a space unveiled in 2019 as a temporary platform for monumental public art commissioned by the High Line. When it opened, it was famously the site of a bronze bust of a Black woman by the artist Simone Leigh, which looked down over 10th Avenue for almost two years.

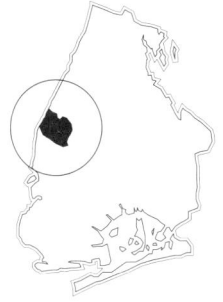

MIDTOWN

With its iconic skyscrapers and countless rows of signs for big name stores, Midtown loves crowds. As the towers vie with one another in height, another side to this concrete jungle can be found in the gardens that lie in their shadows.

The Flatiron Building, elegantly located on the corner of 5th Avenue and Broadway, marks where Midtown begins. This 21-storey skyscraper, which opened in 1902, sets the tone for what you will discover as you progress toward the beating heart of the city. The architecture reflects the frenetic social aspirations of the first generations of New Yorkers, and the landscape was transformed by waves of immigration and the buildings that came in their wake. The industrialists who had made their fortune at the far end of Manhattan Island started moving into tranquil residential areas during the 1800s and the development of Central Park in the second half of the century made the area all the more attractive to wealthy families. Luxury stores and hotels then began to spring up as the streets became lined with increasingly grandiose buildings, along with the skyscrapers. There was also a vibrant cultural scene to entertain these rich patrons at the dawn of the 20th century. The reputation of its theaters, jazz clubs, and bars would carry across the Atlantic.

The Rockefeller Center was built after the stock market crash of 1929 on New York's first large-scale urban construction site, and the complex is testimony to the skills of the architects and associated tradesmen at the height of Art Deco. A brief stroll around the area will reveal other masterpieces in this style that was imported from Europe, including the American Radiator Building, the Chrysler Building, and the Empire State Building. The lines of these architectural achievements would soon be found everywhere from movies to everyday objects as so-called skyscraper style made itself felt in the sitting rooms of aesthetes keen to embrace the avant-garde during the 1930s.

The most recent major construction site has been Hudson Yards at the end of the High Line, with its skyscrapers of modern offices and prestigious apartments, a convention center, and shopping malls to delight a business clientele. The *Vessel*, a ribcage of staircases and viewing platforms with bronze detailing created by the British designer Thomas Heatherwick beside the Hudson, has been attracting the curious to his new neighborhood since 2019. At first blush, this seemingly never-ending mass of concrete, metal, and glass towers can be quite intimidating, especially as it is often accompanied by the roar of traffic and a relentless swarm of pedestrians, but small corners of greenery have found a foothold between the buildings. Verdant spaces like Madison Square, Gramercy Park, and Bryant Park, along with more private gardens, await those keen to take a break from the whirlwind outside. Markets, like the one on Union Square, which is a must, have become places where cultures and generations can meet and mingle, on a human scale.

THE ESSENTIALS

15

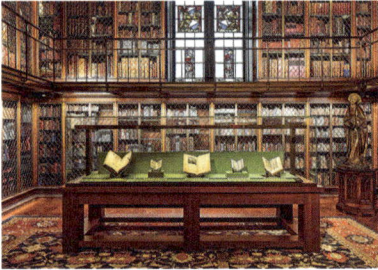

THE MORGAN LIBRARY AND MUSEUM

This institution founded in 1906 conserves rare manuscripts, old books, and works of art.

16

5TH AVENUE

One of the main arteries through Manhattan is famed for its luxury boutiques, museums, and iconic sites such as the New York Public Library.

17

UNITED NATIONS HEADQUARTERS

The headquarters of the UN opened in 1951 and is famously home to the General Assembly and the Security Council.

18

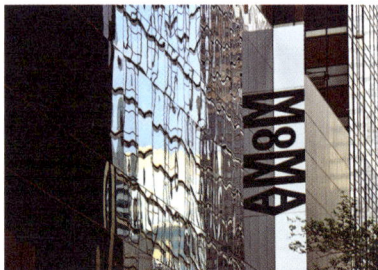

MOMA

This museum founded in 1929 is a global authority on modern and contemporary art, and houses works by Picasso, van Gogh, Warhol, and Pollock.

19

ROCKEFELLER CENTER

This shopping mall and cultural center dating from 1933 houses offices, stores, Radio City Music Hall, and an ice rink (in winter).

20

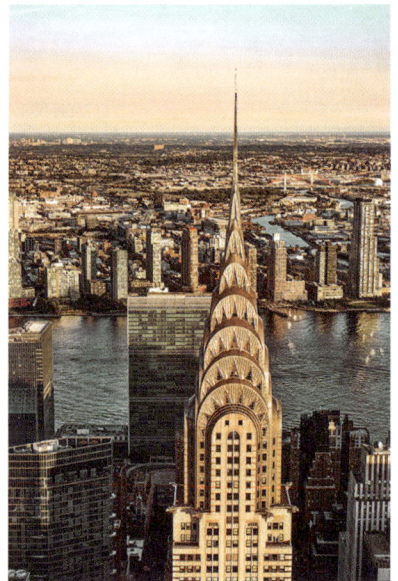

CHRYSLER BUILDING

This Art Deco skyscraper built in 1930 was once the tallest in the world. Its original architecture and stainless-steel spire have become symbols of New York.

21

UNION SQUARE

An iconic square famous for its park and farmers' market, along with its demonstrations, plays a central role in the city's social and cultural life.

22

GRAND CENTRAL TERMINAL

This historic station, opened in 1913, is one of New York's major transport hubs and has become famous for its main hall, the constellations on its ceiling, and its Beaux-Arts-style architecture.

23

NEW YORK PUBLIC LIBRARY

Founded in 1895, this institution is noted for its Beaux-Arts architecture, vast reading rooms, and exceptional collection of books and manuscripts.

24

EMPIRE STATE BUILDING

Rising 1,454 feet (443 m), this iconic skyscraper with its Art Deco architecture was completed in 1931 and boasts some of the most famous panoramic views of the city.

25

BROADWAY

This iconic avenue is the heartland of New York theater, with the most famous playhouses where smash hit musicals are staged.

26

TIMES SQUARE

A bustling junction made famous by its giant screens, theaters, and relentless crowds that has become one of the most iconic symbols of New York.

ABOVE

*The farmers' market that sprang up on Union Square in 1976 has become
a popular meeting place for foodies every Saturday from spring to fall.*

OPPOSITE

*The market stalls overflow with fruit and vegetables brought
in from the New York countryside.*

ABOVE

*Four sculpted limestone portals provide access to the Metropolitan Life Insurance
Company Tower designed in the 1920s by Napoleon LeBrun and Son.*

OPPOSITE

*The architecture of the Metropolitan Life Insurance Company Tower
was inspired by the bell tower on St Mark's Square in Venice.*

EXCURSION

HUSBAND WIFE

SKYSCRAPER LIVING

Living in the sky was a dream fraught with challenges for New York architects and designers, but the Husband Wife studio has dreamed up an interior for an apartment tucked away in the Steinway Tower that combines elegance and comfort rooted in several powerful ideas.

Take the elevator to be safely escorted to the apartment entrusted by an aesthete into the care of Justin Capuco and Brittney Hart, the founders of the Husband Wife interior design studio. As the doors open, visitors get the impression they are stepping out into thin air, which is a rather immediate and worrying experience! The sky itself has dictated the decor, along with the Art Deco building beside which the thinnest tower in the world was erected in 2014. The Steinway Tower at 111 W 57th Street is notable both for its size and remarkably slender profile, with 84 floors that rise to a height 1,428 feet (43 m). This is the kind of architectural feat routinely on display in New York, especially here along so-called Billionaires' Row beside Central Park.

Brittney Hart had to overcome vertigo to work on site, and while it is easy to lose focus in the sky as you stare out into nothingness, the designer and her partner have sought to embed the furniture in this space of 4,300 square feet (400 m²). They have also chosen materials with rich textures, such as wood and fabrics, for the fixtures and fittings. "There is plenty of glass to bring out luster and light. Although we have embedded this element in our decorative language, we wanted to include

other textures on the walls and ceilings to compensate for its transparency and introduce some softness," explains Brittney.

The flow of the design through the apartment is arranged according to cinematographic cues and the palette of colors is linked to its surroundings, and in particular to Central Park, over which the sitting room has a commanding view. "Colors influenced our work," confirms Brittney, who favored neutral and warm tones for the project. "When we finished, which was in the fall, the park had turned into a carpet of orange, gold, and brown leaves. The decor blended into the landscape marvelously." The designers also made sure that each room had its own distinct personality.

By working with artisans and using vintage furniture, the design studio has created a multilayered decor that has a *trompe-l'oeil* effect with a timeless style. "This way of living on a table-top, high in the sky, is special. It is the dream for some New Yorkers, while others would prefer to live in a brownstone," observes Justin, who has been at pains to create an intimate atmosphere here, recalling the most beautiful Hollywood sets of the 1930s.

1/2/ VANTAGE POINT

The discreetly elegant layout
of the space affords a spectacular
view of Central Park and the old
Barbizon-Plaza hotel.

3/ WARM HUES

To decorate the apartment,
Brittney Hart and Justin Capuco
harmonized the palette of colors
with its surroundings.

4/ MATERIAL EFFECTS

Velvet-upholstered chairs designed by
the duo are used in tandem with other
objects in different textures to prevent
the open-plan decor from seeming
too cold.

ABOVE

Patrons of the Bookmarks rooftop bar can enjoy a charming view over
the area's old apartment buildings at dusk.

OPPOSITE

At 1,428 feet (435 m) in height and 56 feet (17 m) wide, the Steinway Tower (on the right)
is one of the pencil towers that have been springing up across the New York skyline.

NATURE

SECRET GARDENS

AMSTER YARD

Amster Yard in the Turtle Bay neighborhood was laid out by the interior decorator James Aster between 1944 and 1946. It is reached via a gateway between nos. 211 and 215 E 49th Street.

ORGANIC LINES

The garden railings in Amster Yard are forged in romantic shapes.

PALEY PARK

The curtain of water in this garden at 3 E 53rd Street drowns out the noise of Midtown.

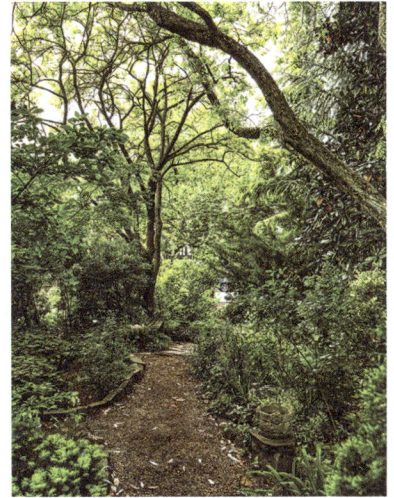

TUDOR CITY GREENS

The two parks on Tudor City Place are part of the city's historic heritage.

GREENACRE PARK

There is a pretty waterfall made up of carved blocks of granite in this green space at 217 E 51st Street.

FORD FOUNDATION

The atrium of the Ford Foundation at 320 E 43rd Street has been turned into a greenhouse of luxuriant vegetation.

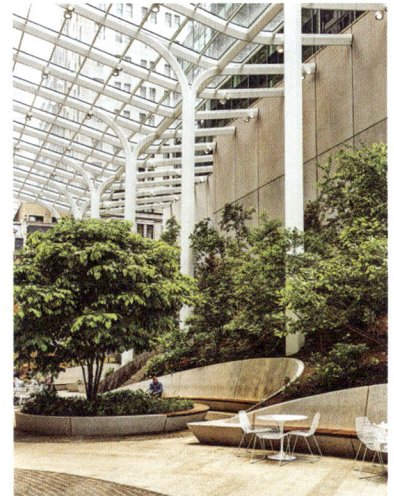

URBAN OASIS

Private individuals have planted flowers to bring a breath of fresh air into the heart of the city.

LIZ CHRISTY GARDEN

This was laid out on the northeastern corner of the Bowery and E Houston Street in 1973 as the city's first community garden.

550 MADISON AVENUE GARDEN

Trees beneath a glass atrium abutting a building.

DEEP DIVE

STEAM HEATING

Many Manhattan buildings have been heated and cooled via a network of underground pipes through which steam has been pumped since 1882. The white fumes that escape from tall orange-and-white stacks in the streets bear witness to the intensity of the energetic action below ground.

Much like yellow cabs, tall orange-and-white stacks topped with thick white vapor have become New York icons. This strange phenomenon, which has been recorded by the greatest photographers and film makers, indicates the presence of a network of pipes distributing high-pressure steam beneath the streets, an underground labyrinth that heats and cools the air in many of Manhattan's tower blocks.

The idea of using fine droplets of water vapor to heat buildings dates back to Roman Antiquity, and this system installed in 1882 includes some 106 miles (170 km) of piping, making it the longest steam heating network in the world. The steam produced by plants along the East River in Manhattan, Brooklyn, and Queens is supplied to more than 1,500 buildings from the Financial District to the southern tip of Manhattan Island, as well as the Upper West Side and Upper East Side, straddling Central Park.

The steam is released from water heated to more than 390°F (200°C) and routed to its destination underground, where it is used in large residential and commercial structures such as office blocks, including the Chrysler Building, Rockefeller Center, Empire State Building, United Nations

Headquarters, and World Trade Center. The 9/11 Memorial also makes use of this ingenious system to prevent the water in its pools from freezing during the major cold snaps that can strike New York during winter.

This source of energy is clean, thanks to the use of water and natural gas to create the precious steam, and has the additional advantage of not obstructing buildings, so it has been adopted by a number of communities. It is used to heat, cool, and even provide water and electric power to schools, churches, hotels, and hospitals, which use it to sterilize medical equipment and for ironing laundry. It also enables museums such as MoMA and the American Museum of Natural History to maintain the level of humidity required to preserve the works housed in their exhibit halls.

The tall orange-and-white stacks scattered throughout the city are temporary chimneys that indicate a leak or work being carried out underground to prevent an explosion. Employees of the Consolidated Edison company, which runs the network, do their best to direct the steam upward to prevent it from restricting visibility for motorists or from scalding pedestrians. It is a necessary evil that is just part of Manhattan's industrial charm.

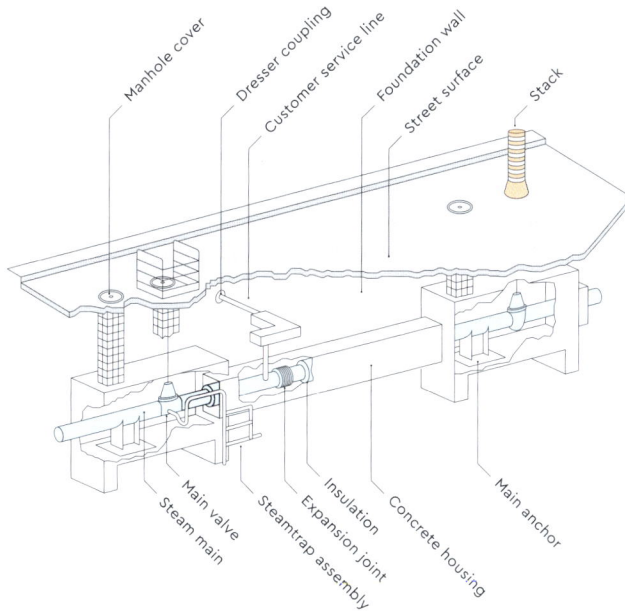

Manhole cover · Dresser coupling · Customer service line · Foundation wall · Street surface · Stack

Main valve · Steam main · Steamtrap assembly · Expansion joint · Insulation · Concrete housing · Main anchor

1/ PIPE NETWORK

New York's steam distribution system enables safe and efficient transport of energy beneath the city.

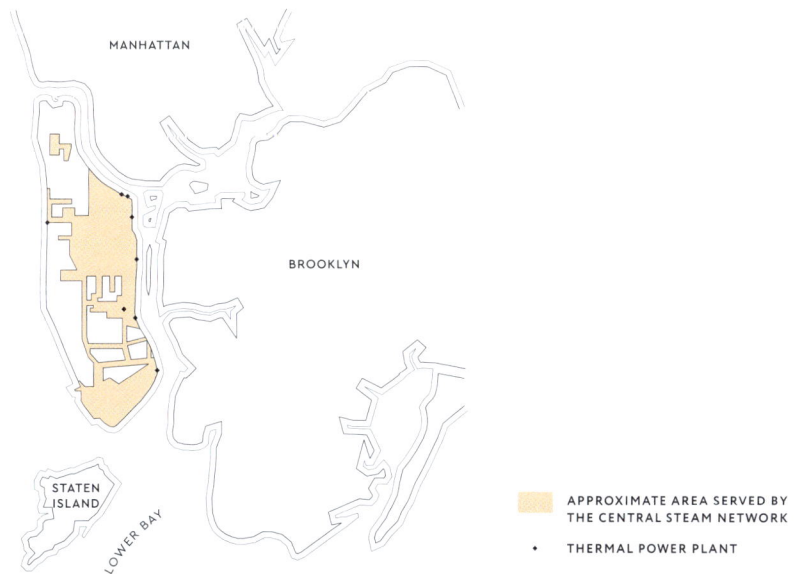

MANHATTAN

BROOKLYN

STATEN ISLAND

LOWER BAY

APPROXIMATE AREA SERVED BY THE CENTRAL STEAM NETWORK

THERMAL POWER PLANT

2/ STEAM DISTRIBUTION IN MANHATTAN

The underground network is used for healthcare purposes, particularly in hospitals, and to heat and cool more than 1,500 buildings, including the Met and the Rockefeller Center.

ABOVE

The fresco Titans and men Working, *designed by José Maria Sert,
adorns one of the Rockefeller Center's great lobbies.*

OPPOSITE

*The elevator doors in the Chrysler Building are decorated with extravagant
marquetry work featuring lotus flowers.*

BRIAN KIM

MICHELIN-STARRED

Brian Kim has opened two restaurants that pay tribute to Korean cuisine in the shadow of the Flatiron: Oiji Mi and, behind it, Bōm. The Michelin-starred chef serves up a sophisticated cuisine in discreet surroundings.

Brian Kim's early years were infused with beauty. Born in Los Angeles to Korean parents, he moved to Seoul at the age of one and traveled widely with his family of entrepreneurs. At the age of nineteen, he was invited by a restaurant-owning uncle on a tour of luxurious destinations in Europe, including art galleries, hotels, boutiques, and restaurants. "We used to change hotel every day to check out the service. I was staggered by the sophistication of the interiors and the local cooking, not to mention the table service that accompanied it," he recounts. As he continued to discover new things, he formulated a strong desire for his later career: to create wonder.

Brian took a course in business studies in pursuit of his goal and then, at the age of twenty-six, opened a restaurant with friends, with no real thought of getting his hands dirty. When the incumbent chef left, he decided to muck in and get involved with this adventure in New York. "I had heard somewhere that if you can make it here, you can make it anywhere," he says with a smile. He learned the rudiments of the job at the Culinary Institute of America and refined his newly acquired skills at Bouley and at Icca in TriBeCa.

True to his original plan, Brian dreamed of providing food lovers with an experience that went far beyond the plate and he opened Oiji Mi, a Korean restaurant in the East Village, in 2015. "There weren't many modern Korean restaurants in the city so I decided to go for it, as a pioneer. I was scared of how the public would react, but the response I got was extraordinary; the reviews were excellent scarcely six months after we opened!" Oiji Mi opened in the Flatiron District in 2022, taking the quality of service up a notch for patrons prepared to enjoy a five-course meal of delicate flavors in Korean-inspired surroundings at a fixed price of 150 US dollars. Since 2023, a more intimate space at the back of the restaurant has offered fourteen dishes dreamed up by this excellent barbecue chef, and there is even a marble counter, in true Korean tradition.

The plates in both locations are skillfully presented and reflect Brian's love of beautiful things. He also continues to draw inspiration from his travels in Korea and beyond. His efforts won almost immediate recognition from the Michelin Guide for his two Flatiron District establishments, and he is passionate about preserving Korea's culinary heritage. He is aiming to introduce new textures and hopes to use more vegetables in his approach. His latest challenge is to open a restaurant in Paris, the city that helped him to refine his taste.

It is a point of honor for Brian Kim to present his dishes as art on plates designed in collaboration with craftspeople.

KOREAN POINTS OF REFERENCE

Oiji Mi's elegant interior incorporates several elements from the chef's homeland, including the *pojagi* (a kind of patchwork) hanging above the bar.

The twelve buildings of the Tudor City complex were developed by the real estate developer Fred F. French
in the hope of revitalizing a neighborhood plagued by criminality in the 1920s.

A bird's-eye view of the Murray Hill area.

ABOVE

*The Pod 39 hotel's colorful roof terrace has incorporated the
red-brick arches of the original building.*

OPPOSITE

*The Murray Hill neighborhood has a certain charm
with its tree-lined streets.*

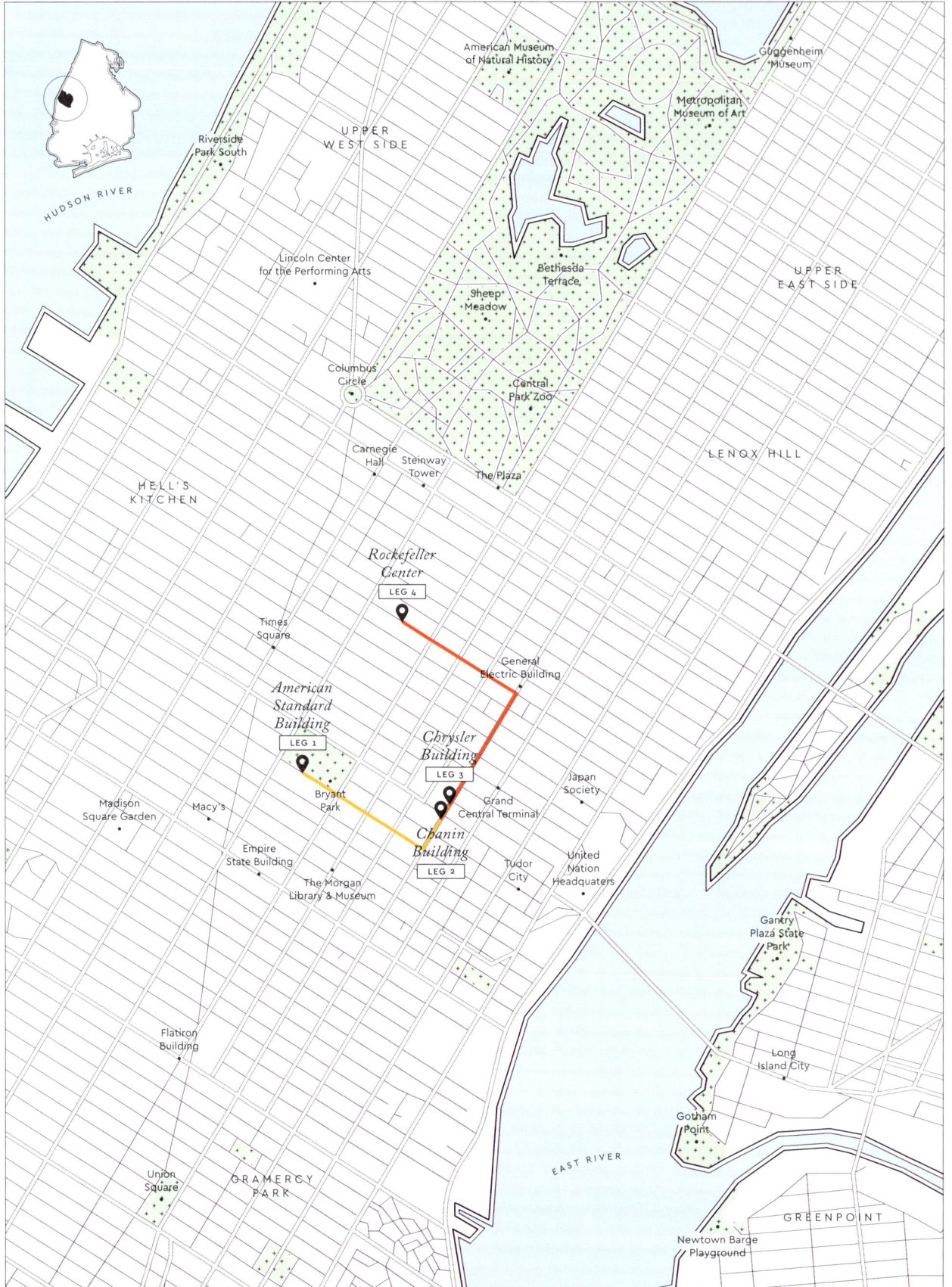

ART DECO GEMS

Art Deco architecture and design were very popular in the New York of the 1920s to the 1940s, and the iconic buildings in this style are worth strolling around in order to inspect them from every angle. New York is home to many masterpieces on a gigantic scale.

LEG 1 : AMERICAN STANDARD BUILDING

The most enjoyable way of exploring this highly visual style is on foot, starting at Bryant Park, which lies opposite the eponymous hotel in the American Standard Building (formerly the American Radiator Building) at 40 W 40th Street. This 23-story building designed by the architect Raymond Hood for a plumbing and heating firm was completed in 1924 as one of the city's first Art Deco constructions. Its black bricks and gold detailing symbolized coal and fire and its silhouette and facade (which was brightly illuminated at night) were to inspire a painting by the artist Georgia O'Keeffe a few years later.

LEG 2 : CHANIN BUILDING

Ten minutes away, at 122 E 42nd Street, stands the Chanin Building, designed by the architects John Sloan and T. Markoe Robertson. The facade of this 56-story tower block next to Grand Central station features a bronze frieze sculpted by Rene Paul Chambellan, with plants and animals to symbolize the evolution of the species. Magnificent chandeliers hang in the entrance lobby and there are many other luxurious details, an opulence prompted by real estate developer Irwin Chanin's visit of the 1925 International Exhibition of Modern Decorative and Industrial Arts in Paris.

LEG 3 : CHRYSLER BUILDING

Many consider the Chrysler Building (just across the road at 405 Lexington Avenue) to be the jewel in New York's architectural crown. This tower block with its steel scales was built by William Van Alen for Walter Chrysler, a captain of the automobile industry, and at the time of its opening in 1930, it was the tallest in the world at 1,046 feet (319 m). The gargoyles, shaped liked eagles' heads, are reminiscent of car radiator caps of the time. The lobby is open to the public although you must stand close to the walls. You will marvel at the sheer elegance, particularly the marble worked in various shades of amber. The elevator doors are inlaid with exotic wood marquetry and lotus flower motifs, a reminder of the influence of Ancient Egypt on the Art Deco movement.

LEG 4 : ROCKEFELLER CENTER

Make a quick detour down to number 570 on the same avenue to admire the General Electric Building and its crown-shaped roof, reminiscent of a Gothic cathedral, before heading to the Rockefeller Center. This complex of fourteen buildings was commissioned by John Davison Rockefeller Jr, the son of the founder of Standard Oil, and constructed during the 1930s by a team of architects led by Raymond Hood and Wallace Harrison. It features a number of frescos, mosaics, and sculptures. Look out in particular for a steel bas-relief by Isamu Noguchi on the former Associated Press tower at 50 Rockefeller Plaza. The view of New York from the Top of the Rock observatory is said to be the best in the city, offering an exclusive perspective on the legendary Empire State Building.

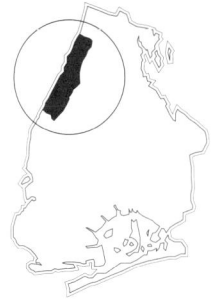

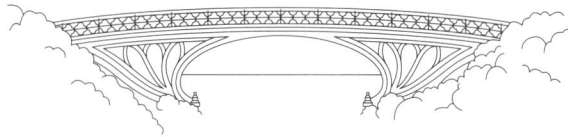

UPPER WEST SIDE

An immense garden was laid out to replace the marshland in the heart of the city in the 19th century and the leafy rectangle of Central Park is now bordered by streets colonized by New York's intellectual and artistic elite. With its old buildings, meticulously maintained brownstones, and exclusive addresses, it is the perfect place for a peaceful stroll.

P.100

*The Oak Bridge was designed by Calvert Vaux in 1860 in an effort to preserve
the rural character of Central Park.*

OPPOSITE

*Inspired by Haussmann, the Ansonia Condominiums completed in 1904
are one of the most remarkable buildings in the city.*

The development of the Upper West Side is closely interwoven with that of Central
Park. The creation of the city's largest garden in 1857 forced many living in
temporary shelters to make way for a gigantic building site, and the social balance
amongst local residents tipped decidedly in favor of the better-off, who continued
to enjoy the peace and quiet of this long strip of land close to the water. The advent
of an elevated steam railroad track in 1870, followed by the metro in 1904, only
accelerated an urban development that was already in progress.

The area forms a narrow strip bounded by Columbus Circle and Columbia University.
The Modernist lines of the Lincoln Center, the cultural icon of the neighborhood,
have overlooked its southern extremity since the 1960s, and this cultural complex
of some twenty performance venues is best known as the home of the renowned
Metropolitan Opera and New York City Ballet.

A favorite haunt of the upper middle classes since its opening, the park has become
a popular destination for all New Yorkers (as well as tourists) thanks to its wide
range of recreational facilities, which even include a zoo. You can still find traces of
the bucolic charm that was its original inspiration, however, and the best time to
visit is during the first hours of the morning before the crowds arrive, when the sun
envelops the bridges and stone sculptures with its golden rays. The view of the
Midtown skyline emerging from the greenery is certainly impressive.

You will see the occasional jogger or dog walker picking their way through the crowds
of strollers en route to prestigious apartment blocks, and any walk along the edge
of the park is enhanced by the eclectic mix of architectural styles, with Beaux-Arts,
Art Deco, and Gothic Revival rubbing shoulders with the Renaissance of The Dakota
Building. This 1884 edifice housed the city's first luxury apartments and former
residents include Lauren Bacall, Humphrey Bogart, John Lennon, and Yoko Ono.
These legendary couples exemplify the local intelligentsia who are still very much a
presence on the Upper West Side. Columbia University, which settled in
Morningside Heights in 1897, helped to reinforce the elitist nature of the area,
and its young and cosmopolitan students now bring a breath of fresh air to the
surrounding residential blocks and shopping streets as they establish a certain
lifestyle. Much like their neighbors, the students are not averse to slipping away to
Riverside Park, a green space beside the Hudson River. Shielded from the throngs
of tourists, it is an ideal place to watch the sun go down.

THE ESSENTIALS

27

THE EL DORADO

This Art Deco residential block boasts
twin towers looking out over Central Park.

28

MUSEUM OF ARTS AND DESIGN

This museum is dedicated to applied arts, design, and contemporary crafts.

29

GRAND BAZAAR NYCA

The market sells a variety of antiques, crafts, and vintage clothes.

30

METROPOLITAN OPERA

The Lincoln Center's opera house opened in 1966 and now stages performances from the classic and modern repertoire.

31

THE DAKOTA

This residential block on 72nd Street was built in 1884 and is noted for its neo-Renaissance architecture and as the residence of John Lennon.

32

ZABAR'S

This delicatessen and caterer is famous for its gourmet produce.

33

THE CATHEDRAL OF ST. JOHN THE DIVINE

This episcopal church on Amsterdam Avenue is one of the largest in the world and has still not been completed since construction began in 1892.

*The spectacle of sunset on the Upper East Side is
one of the joys of a stroll in Central Park.*

ABOVE

Morningside Park boasts beautiful views of the rooftops of Harlem.

OPPOSITE

Romanesque Revival houses reminiscent of fairytale castles stand just a stone's throw from Central Park.

AMERICAN MUSEUM OF NATURAL HISTORY

With its dinosaur skeletons, meteorites, and treasures from the dawn of time, the American Museum of Natural History is an extraordinary place to explore for visitors of any age. Since opening in 1877, it has established itself as one of the most important institutions of its kind in the world.

The naturalist Albert S. Bickmore was passionate about the marvels of the natural world from a young age, and he became the driving force behind a project that was finally realized at the edge of Central Park. Attending lectures given by a Swiss zoologist and biologist at Harvard led him to dream of founding a museum of natural history in New York, and he succeeded in attracting donors and politicians to a cause that came to fruition in 1869, with the cultural institution opening its doors eight years later. Over time, the first edifice, of Victorian style, was joined by a Romanesque Revival building that was then given the Beaux-Arts-style facade now greeting visitors who arrive from the Central Park side. Like a living creature, the museum continued to evolve and become the imposing cultural institution of today.

The museum initially funded expeditions to distant places, enriching its collections with the discoveries they made, before moving on to cooperation with academic institutions such as the adjacent Columbia University to advance knowledge in fields such as paleontology and genetics. The history of the universe is set out in its many exhibit halls; the displays of fossils introduce visitors to the first vertebrates, including dinosaurs and mammoths. There is something to make everyone think, from gemstones to archeological finds.

A gigantic glass cube housing an aluminum sphere was added to the complex in 2000, and the Rose Center for Earth and Space has brought the museum into the modern era. The planetarium installed within this giant ball will take you on a mind-blowing journey through the cosmos.

This push into the future has been continued with a wing opened in 2023 that resembles a beehive or an anthill and houses a new entrance lobby. The architecture of the Richard Gilder Center for Science, Education, and Innovation was designed by Jeanne Gang, a Chicago-born architect, who went to study the canyons and caves of the American West in order to create it. Its reinforced concrete chambers immerse visitors in a subterranean world similar to that inhabited by the insects whose life the museum strives to depict in this new setting. Given what is currently at stake with the climate, highlighting the vital role played by insects in the planet's biodiversity is a project of great use to the public.

1/ A GIANT BEEHIVE

The architect Jeanne Gang dreamed up a structure made of reinforced concrete cells for the Richard Gilder Center for Science, Education, and Innovation.

2/ SILHOUETTES

Mammoth skeletons await visitors of all ages on the fourth floor.

3/ TRACES

Objects fashioned by humans since prehistoric times shed light on our development.

4/ ELEMENTS

Some of the exhibit halls in the museum resemble cabinets of curiosities.

ABOVE

Visitors to the Lincoln Center are greeted by these Henry Moore statues.

OPPOSITE

The Lincoln Center for the Performing Arts was built where West Side Story *was filmed.*

ABOVE

It's easy to forget the hustle and bustle of Manhattan amongst the majestic trees of Central Park.

OPPOSITE

You can go boating on the pond beside the San Remo, a prestigious apartment building built between 1929 and 1930.

Columbus Circle at the junction of Broadway and 8th Avenue marks the starting point of the Upper West Side.

The Mandarin Oriental hotel looks out over Central Park and luxury apartment blocks.

BANH VIETNAMESE SHOP HOUSE

Chef Nhu Ton and her team are hard at work behind the stoves of her restaurant near Columbia University, promoting authentic Vietnamese cooking that reflects the culinary diversity of her homeland.

The kitchen has long been a place of refuge for Nhu Ton, who left Vietnam at the age of twenty-two with a hotel and catering qualification in her back pocket to start a new life in the United States. After a stay in Louisiana, she headed for New York, where the harshness of her daily life as an immigrant put a dent in her enthusiasm. "I couldn't speak English and I didn't have a cent. I felt lost there. Making food from my country was a way of re-establishing a connection with my people." Using only the basic equipment she had available, she set about trying to recreate the dishes from a childhood she had spent with her mother and grandmother, both excellent cooks.

The drive to survive gradually turned into a business proposition and in 2018, she and a partner took over a Vietnamese restaurant in the Bronx. The menu was kept classic to keep a clientele of regulars happy, but a year later, with the support of her partner John Nguyen, Nhu decided to open another outlet to introduce New Yorkers to the full breadth of the dishes from her native country. Her main objective was to break down the prejudices that westerners had about Asian cuisine. "Most Vietnamese restaurants essentially sell pho and bánh mì, but we have plenty of other dishes whose flavors will change depending on how they are marinated or their ingredients are cooked," she points out.

The COVID-19 pandemic delayed the launch of the Bánh Vietnamese Shop House, which is located at 942 Amsterdam Avenue in an area of the Upper West Side that is popular with the Asian community, in particular students from nearby Columbia University. Because of the public health situation, at the end of 2020, Nhu and John decided to open the restaurant as a weekend pop-up. A photo of a dish posted to the restaurant's Instagram account rapidly went viral, the popularity of the establishment grew and grew, and suddenly the chef found herself working night and day. The restaurant has never looked back and many food lovers can generally be found in line, awaiting tasty food at low prices.

The restaurant's interior has tropical touches and an open kitchen that allows diners to soak up the place's creative energy. The menu features delicately flavored soups and dishes, some of which include *bánh*, a sort of fermented rice cake that takes a couple of days to prepare. Nhu goes back to spend at least a month every year in Vietnam to perfect her understanding of local culture through the lens of cooking. In 2025, she and her partner John opened Bánh Anh Em, a new restaurant in the East Village, where base ingredients (such as the noodles used in pho) are prepared. "Food has magical properties, uniting the past and the present", asserts Nhu, whose ambition is to delight and comfort those passing through her doors.

With its simple, cheerful decor and comfort food, the restaurant near Columbia University is a hit with locals.

DISHES

Thanks to Nhu Ton's culinary forays to Vietnam, the menu has tasty surprises in store for diners.

ABOVE

Lovers of old books and vinyl should consider stopping by Westsider Books and Westsider Records at 2246 Broadway.

OPPOSITE

Thomas Neville Sr and George A Bagge took their inspiration from Art Nouveau when designing the cornices of the Cornwall at 255 W 90th Street.

NATURE

THE TREASURES OF CENTRAL PARK

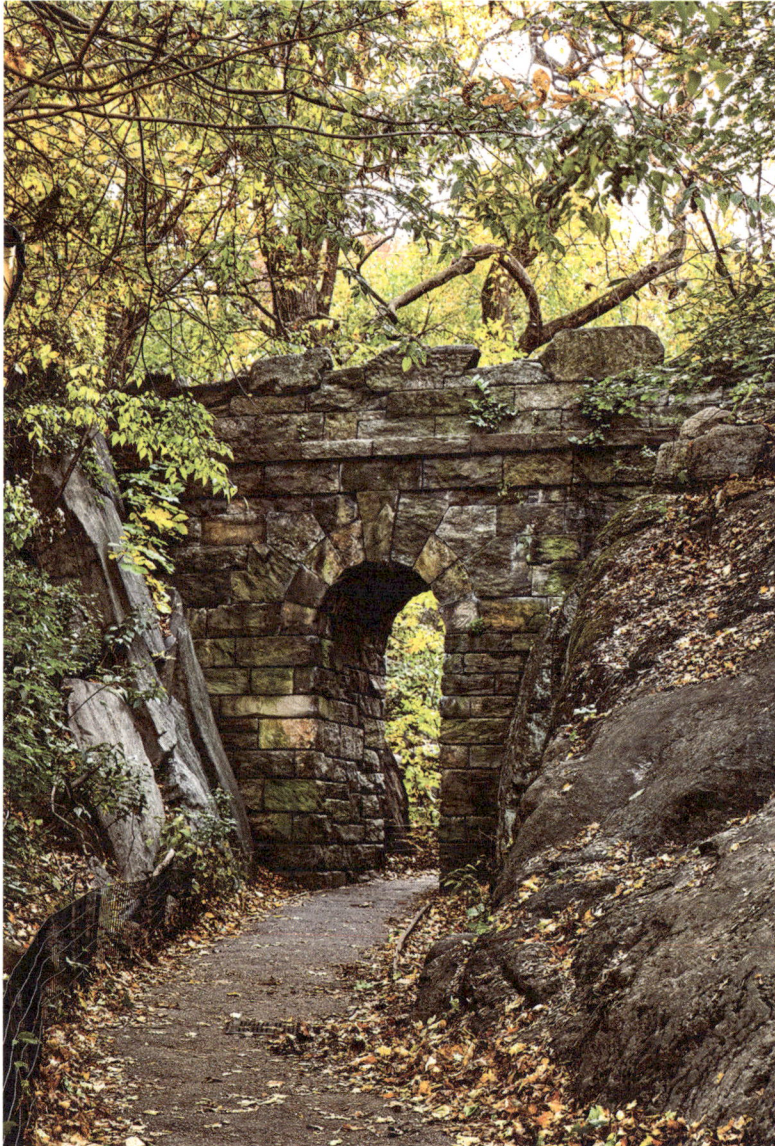

RAMBLE ARCH

Frederick Law Olmsted and Calvert Vaux wanted the landscaping
in the park to look as if it had been created by nature.

PANORAMA

The constantly evolving Midtown skyline can be glimpsed in the distance.

PIONEERS

This statue celebrates the centennial of the ratification of the 19th Amendment, which gave women the right to vote.

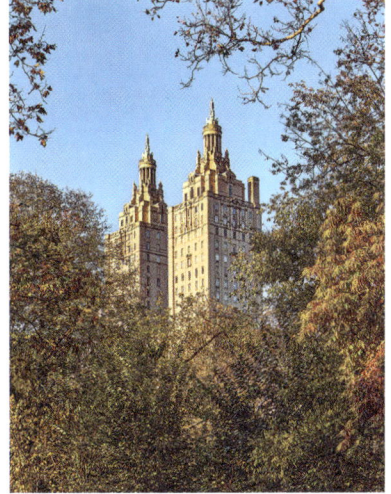

BETHESDA TERRACE

This terrace in the heart of the park is a blend of Romanesque Revival, Gothic, and Classical influences.

THE RESERVOIR

A body of water named after Jacqueline Kennedy-Onassis, who used to walk here.

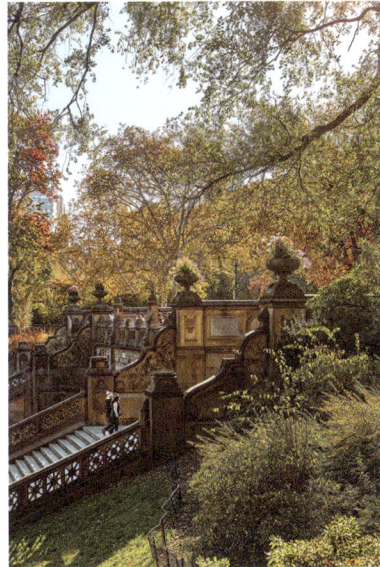

GRANDIOSE

The steps leading up to Bethesda Terrace are carved with motifs representing the four seasons.

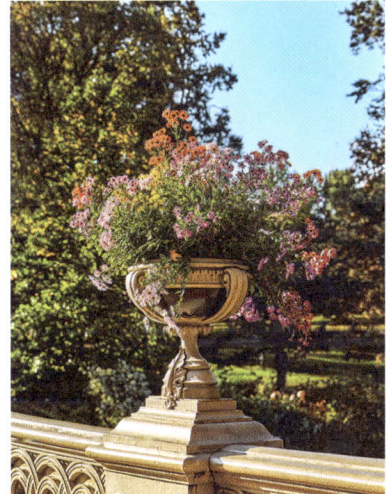

THE SAN REMO

Just one of the legendary apartment blocks in the neighborhood.

BOW BRIDGE

The planters on this Victorian-style cast-iron bridge are bursting with flowers in summer.

THE POND

You can admire the Plaza Hotel from the big boulders and bridge at the entrance to the park.

The Schinasi Mansion on Riverside Drive was used as a location for the
White Collar *TV series.*

The stained-glass windows are just one of the notable features of Riverside Church,
the tallest church in the United States, which was inspired by Chartres cathedral.

DEEP DIVE

BASEBALL
THE NATIONAL SPORT

Baseball, a European import, has become phenomenally popular in New York, achieving an almost cult-like status. Yankee Stadium in the Bronx and Citi Field in Queens are the shrines to a sport adored by fans on every rung of the social ladder.

On August 25, 2024, a jersey in New York Yankees team colors worn by the player Babe Ruth in 1932 was snapped up at auction in Texas for a cool 24.1 million US dollars, which gives some idea of just how important this sport is on American shores. New York parks are used as baseball fields by local clubs, schools, and families.

The origins of this ball game are a subject of controversy. Some claim to have found evidence of it in ancient Egypt and Greece, and although the first references to this sporting discipline, undeniably similar to that of cricket, appear in 18th-century England, it was in the United States that it was first routinely played following the arrival of British immigrants en masse. The rules of the game were laid down by the New York Knickerbocker Base Ball Club in 1845 and sixteen American clubs formed the National Organization of Base Ball Players twelve years later. The first championships could begin.

The equipment used includes a bat made of aluminum or wood, a very hard ball covered in leather or synthetic material sewn with red thread, a leather glove, a helmet and studded boots for pitchers and fielders, and a mask, chest protection, and shin guards for catchers. Two teams of nine players take turns at offense and defense, and each player has a go at hitting the ball with the bat before running between the bases laid out on the field. You score a point (a run) if you manage to go all the way round before the opposing team can retrieve the ball. If you knock it out of the field and render it inaccessible to your opponents, you score a much-vaunted home run, and such an achievement is celebrated by the appearance of a red apple at Citi Field, the stadium of the Mets (the other big baseball team in New York is the Yankees).

Every encounter between the Mets and Yankees draws an impressive crowd to the stadium. It is a family occasion, and people dress up in jerseys and caps with their favorite team's colors and feast on popcorn and hot dogs. The holy grail for any fan is to catch a ball that has been knocked into the stands.

BASEBALL PITCHING

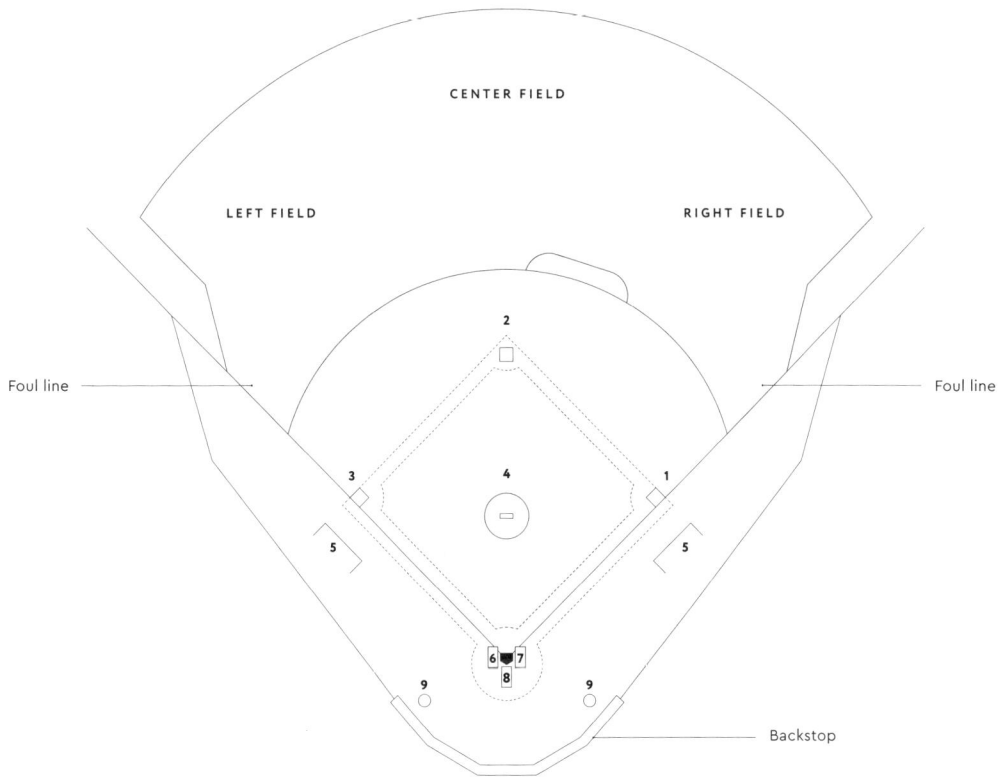

CENTER FIELD

LEFT FIELD

RIGHT FIELD

Foul line

Foul line

Backstop

THE FIELD

1 First base **2** Second base **3** Third base **4** Pitcher
5 Coach's box **6** Right-handed batter's box **7** Left-handed batter's box
8 Catcher **9** On-deck circle

Pitching the ball

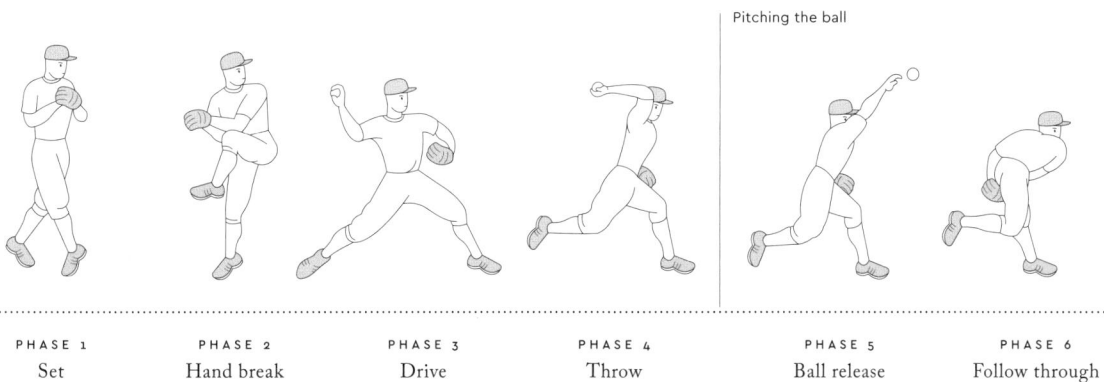

PHASE 1	PHASE 2	PHASE 3	PHASE 4	PHASE 5	PHASE 6
Set	Hand break	Drive	Throw	Ball release	Follow through

ABOVE

Doormen attend to the comfort of residents of buildings on the Upper West Side.

OPPOSITE

*The architecture of the houses in Riverside features a number
of eye-catching details, including this bay window.*

Edgewater

Riverside
State Park

HAMILTON
HEIGHTS

Hamilton Grange
National Memorial

CLIFFSIDE

WEST
HARLEM

HUDSON RIVER

Independence
Harbor

116 St.
Columbia
University Station

LEG 1

Apollo
Theater

Riverside
Drive

LEG 2

Mount Morris
Historic Distric

Morningside
Park

351
Riverside Drive

Cathedral
of St. John the Divine

HARLEM

337
Riverside Drive

MANAHATTAN
VALLEY

Joan
of Arc Monument

LEG 3

The Garden
People

NORTH
MEADOW

EAST
HARLEM

West Side
Community Garden

UPPER
WEST
SIDE

El Dorado

Jacqueline Kennedy
Onassis Reservoir

The Jewish
Museum

A STROLL THROUGH RIVERSIDE PARK

Riverside Park stretches out along the Hudson like a ribbon of green. The promenade was designed by Frederick Law Olmsted, the landscape architect who created Central Park, and opulent homes owned by wealthy New York families and film directors have sprung up alongside it.

LEG 1 : RIVERSIDE PARK

Less frequented by the tourists who prefer Central Park, this green space along the Hudson is a constant in the daily lives of local residents. There is a promenade that links 72nd Street and 158th Street, but leave the subway at 116th Street-Columbia University station and follow the students onto this tree-lined strip of land with its beautiful views of the water and New Jersey beyond. The slightly rugged terrain here prompted landscape architect Frederick Law Olmsted to use rubble from the Central Park construction site to flatten out the land. The English-style park layout was intended to recall the Hudson Valley in the distance, and its multiple levels allow for the integration of vehicle traffic along the banks of the Hudson without spoiling the walk along the city's longest waterfront.

LEG 2 : RIVERSIDE DRIVE

As you stroll along Riverside Drive, the broad avenue looking out over Riverside Park, look up to admire the facades of the apartment buildings and fancy houses alongside. The Schinasi Mansion at number 351 was named for its first owner, who came from Turkey to make a fortune by inventing a cigarette-rolling machine, and stands out from its neighbors with four facades faced with white Vermont marble and Renaissance Revival-style dormer windows. Its layout is the work of architect William Burnet Tuthill, who also designed the Carnegie Hall, and the building was used at the end of the 2000s as a location for shooting the television series *White Collar*, in which art-forger-turned-FBI-asset Neal Caffrey sets up a secret lair in an attic space with a large roof terrace. The impressive red brick and limestone River Mansion at number 337 on the corner of 106th Street was built between 1900 and 1902 by architect Robert D. Kohn, who trained at the *École des Beaux-Arts* in Paris. Much like its neighbors, it reveals a pronounced taste for all things European.

LEG 3 : 91ST STREET COMMUNITY GARDEN

Stroll on for another twenty minutes and, after a quick detour to the bronze statue of Joan of Arc at the end of 93rd Street, stop off at the 91st Street Community Garden (aka the Garden People). This little corner of paradise has been looked after by local gardening enthusiasts since 1981 and it was also used as a location for the final scene of the movie *You've Got Mail* with Meg Ryan and Tom Hanks. This is a magical place when the low sunbeams of a sunny afternoon in the fall shimmer across the last of the flowers.

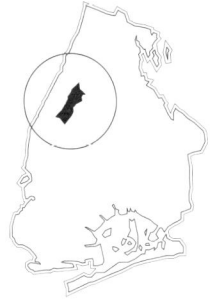

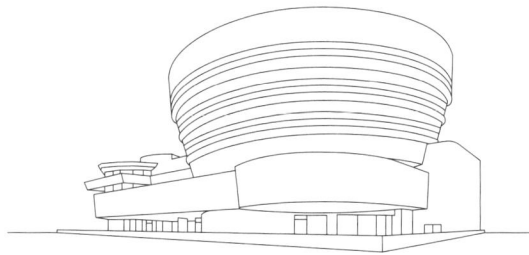

UPPER EAST SIDE

A world away from the hustle and bustle of Midtown, the Upper East Side
is home to luxury stores and mansions built from the great fortunes that helped
the city to boom in the 19th century. Some of these have been turned into museums
where time seems to stand still.

P.132

*The ivy-clad facades lend the streets of Carnegie Hill on the
Upper East Side a touch of Romanticism.*

OPPOSITE

Traffic signals suspended in space have become an icon of the city.

The awnings in front of apartment blocks under which liveried doormen stand ready tell you all you need to know about the levels of sophistication typical of the Upper East Side. The major mass market brands of Midtown give way to a string of luxury boutiques along Madison Avenue and the fancy apartments of the surrounding area. Even the smallest deli demonstrates a pronounced preference for the finer things in life, and these come at a price; living in Marilyn Monroe and Greta Garbo's old neighborhood is a privilege reserved for a certain elite.

The Upper East Side was a vacation spot for early colonists hoping to escape the oppressive summer heat of the city and for a long time it looked like the countryside. There were even a few farms there in the 18th century. The creation of Central Park, which began in 1857, accelerated the transformation of the area alongside the park. Brownstones began to spring up, followed by mansions inspired by the French or Italian Renaissance and destined for families who had made their fortune in industry or finance. A section of 5th Avenue that has become the haunt of the upper middle classes has acquired the nickname Billionnaires' Row.

Most of these lavish residences were replaced by apartment blocks in the 1910s. Those that remained are now home to embassies or have been turned into museums, in particular around the Metropolitan Museum of Art (the Met) where the famous Museum Mile boasts a cultural trail matched by few world cities.

It is fun to let your imagination wander and recreate the past, so look for any excuse to immerse yourself in the New York of yesteryear, like in Bemelmans Bar, the piano bar of the legendary Carlyle Hotel, in which the artist Ludwig Bemelmans painted a faux-naïf fresco in 1947 that depicted Central Park during the four seasons, in exchange for eighteen months of accommodation.

History is everywhere you look along the street front. The white, shell-like facade of the Guggenheim Museum encloses the only building Frank Lloyd Wright, the famous Chicago-born architect and designer, was prepared to build in New York (in 1944) as he hated the vertical development of the city.

On 2nd Avenue an aerial tramway will take you past Queensboro Bridge and on to Roosevelt Island in just a few minutes. The area is not anything particularly special but it does have the advantage of an exclusive view of the Midtown skyline.

THE ESSENTIALS

34

PLAZA HOTEL

This iconic Beaux-Arts hotel on 5th Avenue
famously makes an appearance in *The Great Gatsby*.

35

COOPER-HEWITT, SMITHSONIAN DESIGN MUSEUM

This museum dedicated to the decorative arts has a collection of exhibits from the 18th century to the present day.

36

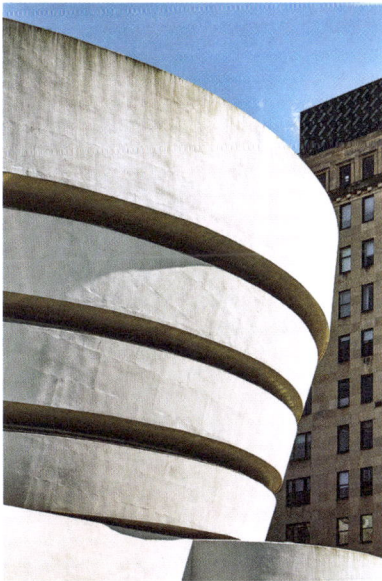

GUGGENHEIM MUSEUM

The architecture of this museum of contemporary art designed by Frank Lloyd Wright is in the form of an inverted spiral.

37

THE FRICK COLLECTION

This museum established in 1935 exhibits mainly European canvases from the 14th to the 19th century.

38

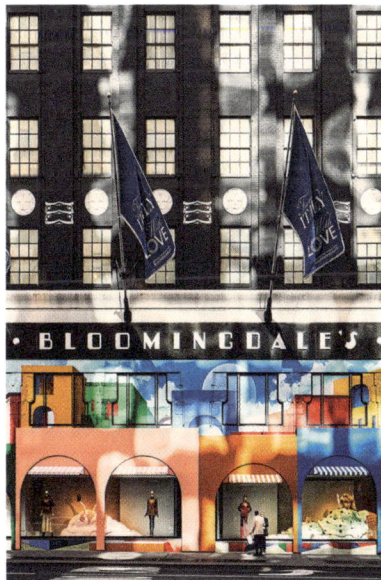

BLOOMINGDALE'S

Founded in 1861, this department store is known for its luxury goods and the display windows it decorates at the end of the year.

39

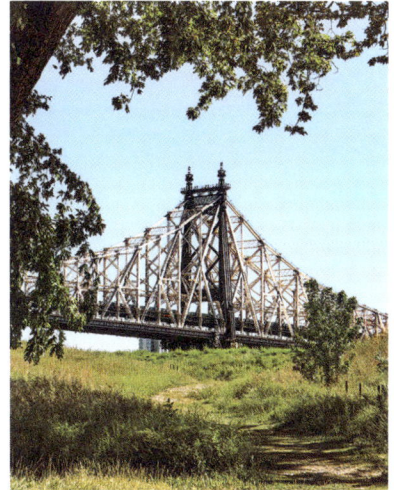

QUEENSBORO BRIDGE

This cantilever bridge with a span of 3,725 feet (1,135 m) was built to link Manhattan and Queens in 1909.

40

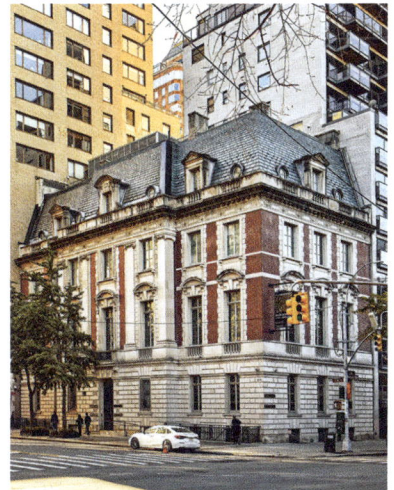

NEUE GALERIE

A museum dedicated to Austrian and German art from the early 20th century (Klimt, Schiele, etc.).

ABOVE

*It is a very short hop to Roosevelt Island
on the tramway.*

OPPOSITE

*This narrow strip of land in the middle of the East River is a mile and
three-quarters (3 km) long and lies between Manhattan and Queens.*

Dry cleaners and elegance are both the norm and go hand in hand.

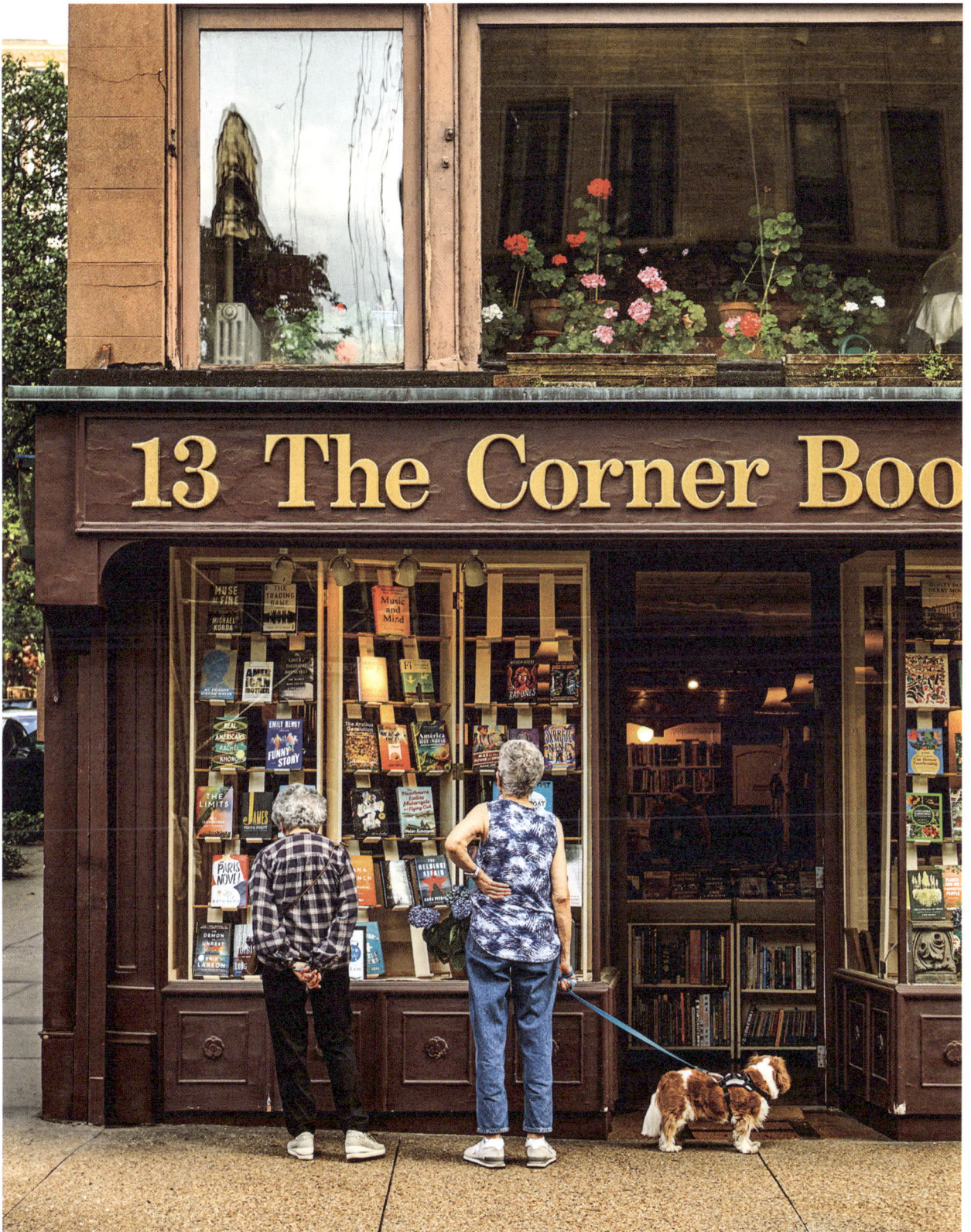

*The old-fashioned charm of the Corner Bookstore has
made it a hit with Carnegie Hill residents.*

THE METROPOLITAN MUSEUM OF ART

Whether you come here to explore the artistic treasures of the world starting from Ancient Egypt, to seek inspiration, or to be intoxicated by beauty, the Metropolitan Museum of Art (the Met) is an endless source of wonder.

Since opening its doors in 1870, the Met has welcomed visitors of every kind. Visitors include families, students, researchers, authors, budding artists, established talents, and celebrities from the worlds of fashion or film, especially on the occasion of its annual gala in May in support of the Costume Institute, which is part of the institution. Enter the Met and prepare to encounter a thousand and one fascinating exhibits.

It is a wise move to forget about exploring this immense museum in its entirety in a single day, as it houses more than two million works. The intention behind the collection, which was assembled by a group of artists and patrons, was to create a space dedicated to art modeled on the museums of Europe. It was initially housed on 5th Avenue in Midtown before a building of the size of this ambitious project could be built on Central Park. The Beaux-Arts-style facade looking out over 5th Avenue was constructed in 1902, and many other additions have come together to create a sprawling cultural hub that is one of the most popular museums in the world. Every culture from pre-history to the 20th century is represented here, and the must-sees for your first visit should include the collection of Ancient Egyptian art and the Temple of Dendur commissioned by the Roman emperor Augustus around 23 BCE, the collection of art from Africa, the Americas, and Oceania, with its gigantic totems, and the European paintings and sculptures that include a host of masterpieces by the likes of Vermeer, Picasso, Monet, and Van Gogh.

The American wing of the museum also houses creations by artisans, architects, and designers, such as a living room entirely designed by Frank Lloyd Wright, whose notion of "total art" had a profound influence on modern domestic interiors, and furniture of meticulously calculated functionality by the Shakers, members of an 18th-century religious community now considered the founders of American design.

More than century and a half after its creation, the Met continues to call upon the genius of contemporary artists as it reinvents itself. In 2014, it invited Stephen Alesch and Robin Standefer, founders of the famous New York architecture and design studio Roman and Williams, to revamp the decor of its British galleries for their reopening in 2020. The space, which is next to the immense hall of medieval art, is decorated with arches that echo those in the room next door and a gigantic display case houses several hundred porcelain teapots from the 18th and 19th centuries that had been unearthed from the museum's storage; yet another extraordinary encounter.

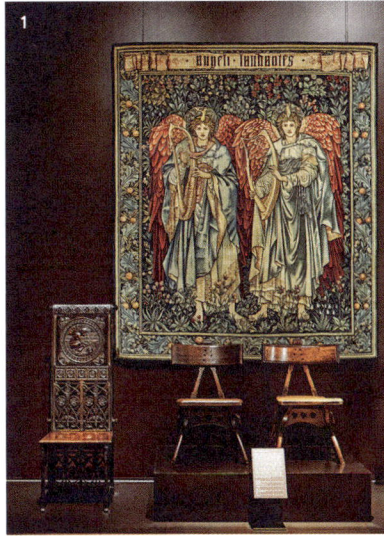

1/ ATMOSPHERE

The Roman and Williams design studio reimagined the decor of the British galleries, favoring dark hues.

2/ EGYPTIAN ART

The section devoted to Egyptian antiquities on the first floor is one of the finest in the world.

3/ GREEK ANTIQUITIES

Aesthetes and artists are drawn to the many Greek sculptures here.

4/ TEMPLE OF DENDUR

This temple built in 23 BCE for the Roman emperor Augustus is the centerpiece of the section dedicated to Egyptian art.

5/ TEA TIME

The British galleries house an impressive collection of teapots.

*The streets of Lenox Hill are lined with prestigious houses dating from the early 20th century,
some of which have balconies and bay windows made of patinated metal.*

VILLA ALBERTINE
A CULTURAL MELTING POT

Once a private mansion house, Villa Albertine on 5th Avenue is a cultural center with a bookstore that promotes interaction between French and American authors, inviting them to expand the horizons of their contemporaries.

To set the scene, there is a bronze sculpture of Antoine de Saint-Exupéry's Little Prince designed by the artist Jean-Marc de Pas that stands at the entrance to the garden of Villa Albertine at 972 5th Avenue. Welcome to a bastion of French culture in the heart of New York, which has famously featured in so many stories and been the favorite haunt of countless authors! This elegant residence, one of the last remaining mansions from the Gilded Age, was the work of architect Stanford White, who also designed the triumphal arch in Washington Square. It was constructed between 1902 and 1906 as a wedding present from Oliver Hazard Payne, sometime treasurer of the Standard Oil Company, for his nephew, William Payne Whitney.

The Italian Renaissance-inspired building has housed the French embassy's cultural mission to the United States since 1952, and the bookshop was opened in 2014. A cupid standing on a fountain at the entrance points the way for visitors, although the original marble statue, which was attributed to Michaelangelo in 2009, is now in the Met. Pass by a room designed as a hall of mirrors by Stanford White and at the end of the corridor you will find the bookstore, whose reverential atmosphere provides a peaceful moment before a museum visit.

The interior, created by designer Jacques Garcia, was modeled on a large, French-style private library, with wooden shelves, leather sofas, and elaborate light fittings to blend into the style of the old mansion. Of particular note, however, is the impressive fresco on the ceiling, depicting the constellations of the zodiac rather like the one in the music room at Villa Stuck in Munich. Busts of historic French and American luminaries such as Benjamin Franklin, Molière, Alexis de Tocqueville, and René Descartes, designed at the École du Louvre, reinforce the historic feel of the place.

The bookstore boasts more than 14,000 volumes in French and English and likes to organize exchanges between writers in French and English to stimulate ideas in a French cultural tradition that dates back to the century of the Enlightenment. Villa Albertine has been hosting artists and designers in residence since 2021, and some of the creations they have left behind can be admired amongst the marble Ionic columns of the majestic entrance lobby, which overlooks Central Park.

1/ THE CELESTIAL VAULT

A fresco depicting the constellations of the zodiac has been painted
on the ceiling of the story given over in part to children's books.

2/ ICON

Visitors are greeted by a
sculpture of the Little Prince.

3/ PRESTIGE

Marble columns are a reminder of
the wealth of the former owners.

4/ DETAILS

A vintage bookcase is perfect for
displaying a selection of books.

ABOVE

The egg creams (a drink made with vanilla ice cream, carbonated water, and cola) at the Lexington Candy Shop have made a name for the establishment.

OPPOSITE

The juicy hamburgers at JG Melon's diner have been attracting locals to 1291 3ʳᵈ Avenue since 1972.

FOOD TO GO

There are so many places to eat in the metropolis, but you should also consider exploring local cuisine in venues other than restaurants. Head for the streets and outlets where you can grab a bite to eat on the hoof without slowing down your exploration of the city.

With their gleaming facades and neon signs, diners have become part of the furniture, and it is impossible to visit New York without visiting one, whether for a brunch of fluffy pancakes or a lunch of juicy hamburgers washed down with a creamy milkshake. The service is speedy and the declared intent is to fill you up. The decor is routinely made up of faux-leather banquettes, sturdy tables, and authentic unpretentious counters that add a touch of retro to the mix. New Yorkers make a point of reserving a table several days in advance to avoid the ignominy of waiting in the streets outside the most popular places, especially at weekends.

If you are short on time, stop off at one of the many delis so beloved of local New Yorkers. These are something between a caterer, bakery, and corner grocery store, and are great places to explore the delicacies inherited from the many foreign communities represented in New York, in particular the large Jewish population with its lox and bagels and smoked meat sandwiches. There are sometimes a few tables, stocked with ketchup and mustard, for dining in-house. Long lines are common.

Sometimes picturesque or even iconic with their striped awnings, the bodegas of New York are similar to the local grocery stores of Europe, and it is here you will find a selection of options to assuage hunger in between museum visits or after a show. Some sell salads, bread from artisan bakers, or even chocolates from local factories to round off your lunch with something sweet. Their main advantage is that they stay open very late.

Street vendors have always been known for their inventive spirit. Horses once pulled carts of street food before the automobile broke new ground for this kind of catering, and now the city boasts countless food carts and food trucks that are mini mobile kitchens. You can get takeout meals from every corner of the globe, sometimes even made by young restaurant owners who have shied away from commercial rents. For better or worse, street food has become a permanent part of New York culture, as evidenced by the hot dog-eating competition that is organized annually on the Fourth of July by Nathan's fast food restaurant in Coney Island.

FOOD CARTS

These sell hot dogs, pretzels, coffee, and sometimes even full meals with a garnish to the pedestrians that hurry past on the streets of Manhattan.

DELIS

Katz's Deli is a New York institution famous for its pastrami sandwiches.

BODEGAS

Bodegas sell a wide selection of produce, from snacks to salads, in every neighborhood of the city.

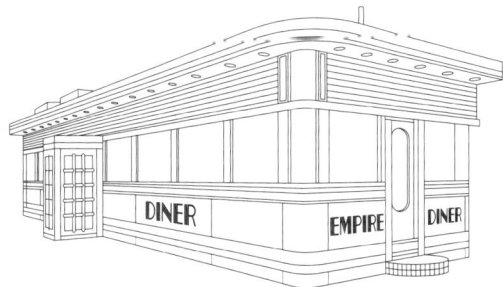

DINERS

A menu of staples and a warm welcome make these unmissable.

WIDE VARIETY

There is no shortage of places to eat in almost every New York neighborhood, with food carts (or trucks), bodegas, delis, cafés, diners, and luncheonettes competing to satisfy your hunger, all at speed.

ABOVE

*Breakfast at Café Sabarsky offers a relaxed taste of the pace of life
on the Upper East Side.*

OPPOSITE

*Many of the brownstones near 5th Avenue were demolished at the end
of the 19th century to make way for lavishly decorated mansion blocks.*

EXCURSION

YORKVILLE

LIFE IN REVERSE

YORKVILLE

This neighborhood to the east of 3rd Avenue, to which many German immigrants
flocked from the 19th century to the 1960s, is named after York Avenue.

DAVID'S BARBER SHOP

Vintage bubble gum dispensers have been installed in front of this barber shop window.

SCHALLER & WEBER

Schaller & Weber sells a wide range of German sausages and is a real institution in the neighborhood.

GAZETTE

There is a European flavor to the food at Gazette.

MILANO MARKET

This deli was founded by an Italian who came to seek his fortune in New York in 1972.

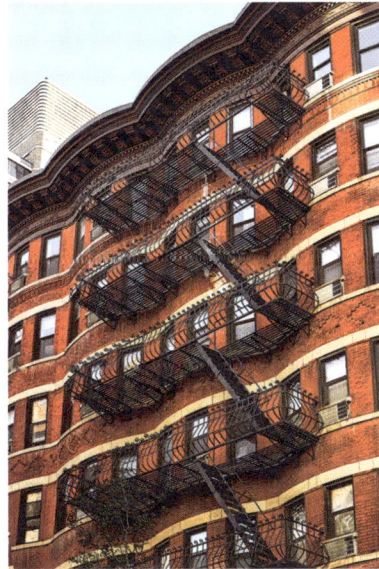

NEIGHBORS

The area is attracting an increasing number of families thanks to the opening of a new subway line on Second Avenue.

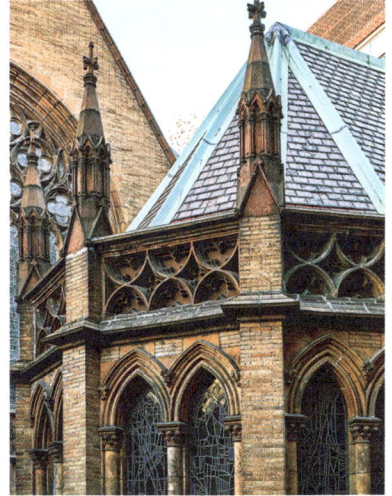

HOLY TRINITY

This church's architecture is reminiscent of a Renaissance French chateau.

FIRE!

You will still see the occasional old fire alarm in some of the streets in the neighborhood.

NESTS

The walls of some homes are covered in greenery.

A doorman keeps watch outside the Lotos Club, a very old literary club.

The Gothic facade of this apartment block built in 1906 is an architectural marvel to be admired after a stroll in Central Park.

ABOVE

*A liveried doorman stands ready outside one of the first residential buildings
designed for upper-class New Yorkers.*

OPPOSITE

*Opulence is the default option around the Metropolitan Museum of Art
(the Met) on 5ᵗʰ Avenue.*

ABOVE

The rocks of Cedar Hill in Central Park are the perfect place to sit for
a moment in the sun.

OPPOSITE

Enjoy a fantastic view of the rooftops of the Upper East Side from the tramway
connecting Manhattan and Roosevelt Island.

HUDSON RIVER

Riverside

West Side
Community Garden

El Dorado

UPPER
WEST SIDE

Jacqueline Kennedy
Onassis Reservoir

American Museum
of Natural History

Metropolitan
Museum of Art

*Cooper-Hewitt,
Smithsonian
Design Museum*

LEG 4

*Neue
Galerie*

LEG 3

YORKVILLE

*Ukrainian
Institute*

Lincoln Center
for the Performing Arts

Bethesda
Terrace

Sheep
Meadow

UPPER
EAST SIDE

Columbus
Circle

Central
Park Zoo

*Park
Avenue
Armory*

LEG 2

*The Plaza
Hotel*

LEG 1

LENOX HILL

HELL'S
KITCHEN

Times
Square

Rockefeller
Center

Roosevelt
Island

MIDTOWN
EAST

Bryant
Park

Chrysler
Building

Japan
Society

Empire
State Building

Freedom
Plaza

Gantry
Plaza State
Park

MIDTOWN

Flatiron
Building

EAST RIVER

LONG
ISLAND CITY

ON THE TRAIL OF THE GILDED AGE

New York's upper classes began to build lavish homes at the end of the 19th century, and the ensuing Gilded Age, an era of economic prosperity brought about by the Industrial Revolution, saw the advent of very ornate houses, some of which still stand to this day.

LEG 1 : THE PLAZA HOTEL

The wonders begin with the Plaza Hotel at 768 5th Avenue, opposite Central Park, and this eighteen-story building constructed in 1907 was inspired by the castles of the French Renaissance. It was the work of Henry J. Hardenbergh, the architect of the Dakota building and the first Waldorf-Astoria, and is notable for its reception lobbies and suites intended for wealthy families. Nowadays, the best approach is to reserve (several months in advance) a table for afternoon tea under the large glass atrium of the Palm Court, which was renovated by Thierry Despont in 2013. Step inside and you will find yourself in the midst of a high society soirée of yesteryear, complete with corsets, trains, and tiaras of the kind depicted in the American TV series *The Gilded Age* (a term that referred to the plating used on jewelry).

LEG 2 : PARK AVENUE ARMORY

Stroll north beside Central Park for about fifteen minutes before taking a right and you will see a red, fortress-like building looming over Park Avenue. This former military building at number 643 was built in a Gothic Revival style in 1880 for the 7th Regiment of the National Guard, whose ranks included many soldiers from prominent families such as the Vanderbilts and the Roosevelts. Within is a club whose lounges boast rich paneling, frescos, and opulent chandeliers. It was saved from demolition in the 2000s by the Swiss architecture practice Herzog & de Meuron and is open to the public for temporary events such as exhibitions or antiques fairs.

LEG 3 : NEUE GALLERY

Head back to 5th Avenue and continue north along Central Park. When you reach E 79th Street, look to the right and admire the ornate facade of the Ukrainian Institute of America with its Gothic and Renaissance-style lines. Continue north for another seven blocks and head right to reach the Neue Gallery at no. 1048. This Beaux-Arts-style building was based on the place des Vosges in Paris by Carrère and Hastings (the architects of the New York Public Library) and was once the home of the Miller family. Since 2001, it has been home to works of art from Germany and Austria, including canvases by Gustav Klimt and furniture by Josef Hoffmann. Don't forget to take a break at the Café Sabarsky, named for the cofounder of the museum and clearly inspired by the cafés of Vienna.

LEG 4 : COOPER-HEWITT, SMITHSONIAN DESIGN MUSEUM

Continue north along 5th Avenue and take a right at E 91st Street, where you will find a museum dedicated to design. The old Gothic Revival mansion that steel magnate Andrew Carnegie moved into in 1902 has sixty-three rooms, and the Cooper-Hewitt Design Museum has been in residence since 1976, exhibiting the collections amassed by the granddaughters of the industrialist Peter Cooper. Its ornate wooden cabinets are an ideal showcase for exhibitions that celebrate the skills of the past and present with creations from the cutting edge of young American design talent.

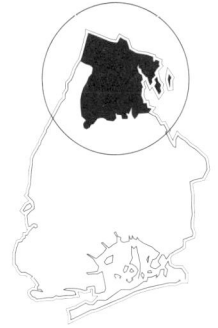

HARLEM & THE BRONX

The boroughs of Harlem and the Bronx lie on opposite banks of the Harlem River on the edge of the city. The former is the cradle of African-American culture, full of places in which to engage with a vibrant artistic community, while the charms of the latter include its retro neighborhoods and green waterside spaces. Both are full of authenticity.

The small village of Harlem, founded in 1658 by Peter Stuyvesant, the first governor of the Dutch colony of New Amsterdam, had long been popular with wealthy New Yorkers as a place in which to enjoy a break in its beautiful homes, but the extension of the elevated train in 1880, linking the area to the center of the city, whetted the appetite of real estate developers. Having built homes here that were intended for the white middle classes, they found that buyers were difficult to come by and opened them up for rent to Black families. The racism that was rife at the time resulted in the departure of existing residents for other neighborhoods. Rents were raised to compensate for these losses, forcing Black families to cram into apartments that would be neglected by their owners. Harlem was slowly becoming a ghetto.

Some of the architectural gems from the urban development at the end of the 19th century have survived. Strivers' Row between 7th and 8th Avenues on 138th Street is lined with brownstones designed by renowned architects, and peaceful corners like this and the historic district of Sugar Hill now attract new residents arriving from Manhattan and Brooklyn.

The history of Harlem is also one of a Black renaissance, a cultural movement between the wards propelled by talents (Duke Ellington, Louis Armstrong, Josephine Baker amongst them) who distanced themselves from the racist stereotypes applied to the artistic community to assert their own identity. This ferment of creativity can still be felt today in the gig venues, bars, and restaurants, where New Yorkers like to gather for brunch and some jazz on the weekend. The Studio Museum on 125th Street in Harlem is both an artistic outlet and a meeting place for this vibrant community.

The Bronx takes its name from Jonas Bronck, the Swede who built Bronck's farm here in 1639. Much like Harlem, the borough is fraught with glaring inequality and high levels of criminality, and while some areas are best avoided, you will discover an authenticity that is sometimes lacking in Manhattan. Little Italy in the Belmont neighborhood offers a small taste of the sweetness of the past, and a visit to the Bronx should include the natural environment that has incredibly been preserved from urban development. The Botanical Garden (the largest in New York), the enclave of Riverdale, and the gardens of Wave Hill on the Hudson, are all lovely spots that visitors, and even some New Yorkers, overlook all too easily.

THE ESSENTIALS

41

NEW YORK BOTANICAL GARDEN

This 250-acre (100-ha) botanical garden laid out in 1891 contains more than a million plants,
a primary forest, and greenhouses inspired by the Crystal Palace in London.

42

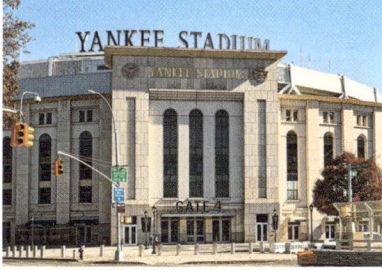

YANKEE STADIUM

The home ground of the New York Yankees opened in 2009 and now hosts soccer games, boxing matches, and major concerts.

43

MOUNT MORRIS HISTORIC DISTRICT

This historic area of Harlem is notable for its 19th-century brownstones, Renaissance Revival buildings, and historic churches.

44

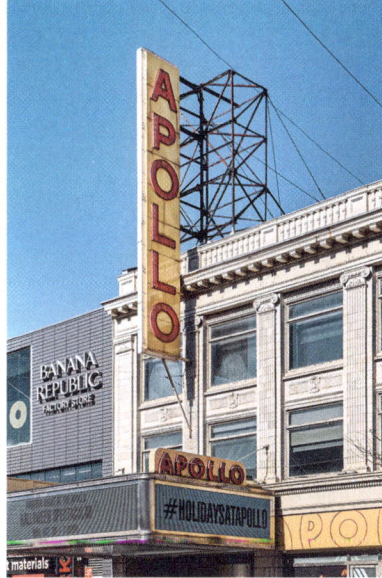

APOLLO THEATER

This iconic Harlem venue opened in 1914 and played a key role in promoting African-American artists.

45

PARK PLAZA APARTMENTS

A residential block built at 1005 Jerome Ave in 1929 and the first Art Deco building to appear in the Bronx.

46

LITTLE ITALY

This neighborhood is the historic epicenter of the Bronx's Italian-American community and is still a destination for Italian food in New York.

47

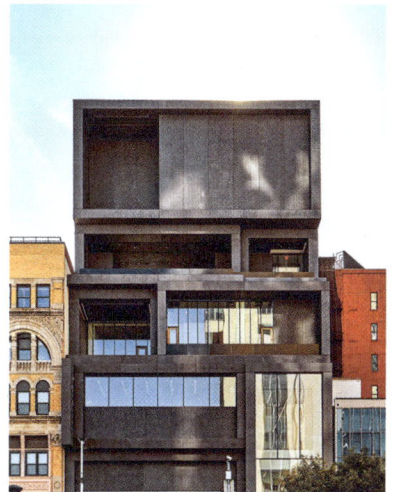

STUDIO MUSEUM

This museum dedicated to African-American art has just been redesigned with new architecture inspired by its surroundings.

ABOVE

Carnivores and vegetarians alike can enjoy a hamburger, fries, and a lemonade or milkshake from Harlem Shake at 100 W 124th Street.

OPPOSITE

Harlem Shake's retro interior is reminiscent of American diners from the 1950s.

ABOVE

The Greater Refuge Temple in the heart of Harlem was once a casino before becoming a theater. You can't miss its multicolored facade.

OPPOSITE

Sugar Hill's rich architectural heritage is a draw for the families who settle here from Manhattan and Brooklyn.

PORTRAIT

ANNA GLASS
DANCE THEATRE OF HARLEM

The Dance Theater of Harlem (DTH) has played an important role in showcasing the contemporary Black arts scene in the United States and across the globe. Anna Glass, the Executive Director of this creative hub, is hard at work giving local young talent wings.

As a child, Anna Glass was happy to lose herself in dance moves in the family home in suburban Detroit. "My mother would watch me gyrating around her. She signed me up for dance classes when I was five," she remembers. Anna was fascinated by the elegance of ballerinas and joined a ballet company. A degree in history of art and law took her down a different path, but the deep love she gained for this artistic discipline during her years of training never left her, nor did the grace that is so noticeable at first sight.

Since 2015, Anna has overseen the management of the Dance Theater of Harlem in the north Harlem neighborhood of Sugar Hill. It is her aim to uphold the legacy of Arthur Mitchell, its founder, who became the first Black dancer to join the New York City Ballet in 1955. The 1968 assassination of the African-American pastor Martin Luther King, one of the leaders of the civil rights movement in the United States, spurred the Harlem-born dancer to embrace his mission and, a year later, he founded a school of dance. As young Black people had been excluded from this artistic milieu, he decided to make access easier for them. "Many people in Harlem were living in poverty back then, because the community had been neglected by the government. Arthur Mitchell was convinced that children could learn discipline and perseverance through this art form and gain a belief in themselves and their ability to become successful citizens," explains Anna.

The ballet company founded in the school has toured the world, with highlights including Nelson Mandela's 1992 invitation to South Africa and its 2026 *Fire Bird* show in Paris. There is still much at stake for Black dancers who routinely face discrimination, and there is no lack of examples. Students have to apply foundation to give their pointe shoes a color close to their own skin tone as the ballet tradition imported from Europe insists on pale shades. "In a performance, a dancer has to make a continuous line, from head to toe. I think they were long excluded from ballet companies because they stood out," explains Anna.

The entire Harlem community is able to enjoy the DTH's creative energy, notably at the Sunday matinees for which its dancers and other artists from the neighborhood perform at very affordable prices. It also works with the Apollo Theater to put on shows and it is a point of honor to participate in parades (including African Day Parade on the third Sunday in September) and other street festivals in Harlem.

Anna Glass, the Executive Director of the DTH, is working to preserve the ballet school at 466 W 152nd Street in the Sugar Hill neighborhood.

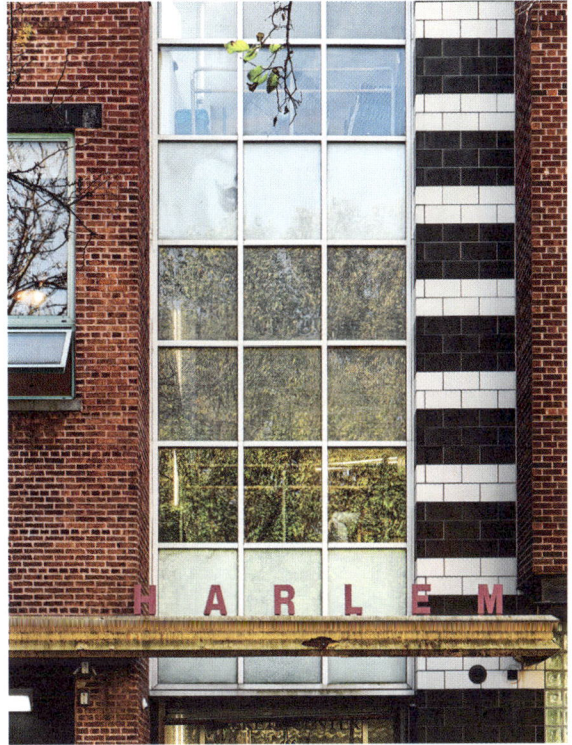

TONE ON TONE
Underlying everything, pointe shoes dyed with foundation to blend them in with the dancers' silhouettes.

The Italian grocery stores on Arthur Avenue in the Bronx sell imported products so that the descendants of immigrants can reproduce the recipes handed down by the generations.

Egidio Pastry in Little Italy, a vibrant neighborhood in the Bronx, has been upholding Italian traditions (and selling biscotti) since 1912.

ABOVE

Orchids bloom in an atmosphere reminiscent of an equatorial rainforest
in the greenhouses of the New York Botanical Garden.

OPPOSITE

The paths lined with cacti and succulents in the Enid A. Haupt Conservatory
recreate the arid ecosystem of the desert.

THE MET CLOISTERS

This hilltop museum in Washington Heights looks like a fortified monastery from the Old World. It is a perfect setting, a world away from the modernity of the city below, for exploring the art and architecture of the Middle Ages.

American sculptor and Rodin enthusiast, George Grey Barnard took on an unusual quest at the turn of the 20th century, making use of the time he spent in the countryside of France to source sculptures and architectural fragments from the medieval period. As World War I loomed, he opened a museum in northern Manhattan to display the items he had brought back to an American audience, and in particular to sculptors, whose imaginations he wished to nurture. The artist did not have the funds to complete his project, however, and had to put his treasures up for sale.

The New York industrialist John D. Rockefeller, a generous patron of the arts, donated a sum of money to the Metropolitan Museum of Art in 1925 to buy the collection, which he subsequently expanded with other works in his possession. He followed this up with an offer of a tract of land along the Hudson River on which to build a museum of medieval art, which opened its doors to the public in 1938. The institution, a rather incongruous sight in New York City, took its name from the fragments of cloisters that had been imported from Europe.

The museum is laid out around reconstructed cloisters through which visitors can track the development of Romanesque and Gothic styles over the centuries. The museum's architecture is evocative of religious buildings from the 12th to the 15th century, and a peaceful stroll takes you past serried ranks of medieval works of art. One must-see curiosity is the famous *Hunt of the Unicorn* tapestry series, woven in Belgium at the turn of the 15th century, but there are also stained-glass Gothic windows, illuminated manuscripts, sacred sculptures, and liturgical items in gold, silver, and ivory, bearing witness to the wealth of the religious heritage of medieval Europe.

Gardens laid out according to descriptions in medieval botanical books also help visitors to imagine life in monasteries of that period, where working the land was a way of living a life of contemplation. Plants once used for their healing properties or prized for their symbolic value now bloom in these green spaces surrounded by stonework.

The modern museum is of great value to art historians and plays an essential role in the study of medieval art in the United States. It is equally prized by architects, designers, artisans, and artists because of the traditional skills it preserves and for its vast collection of everyday images. The avant-garde is all the more captivating when juxtaposed with the legacy of the past, as illustrated by the ancient tapestries that adorn the most audacious interiors in this city.

The museum was constructed on
a hill in Washington Heights overlooking
the Hudson River.

THE CUXA CLOISTER

This cloister was rebuilt using
architectural fragments sourced from the
South of France.

ABOVE

*The shaded arcades of the Cloisters Museum invite visitors
to slow things down.*

OPPOSITE

*The museum is located in Fort Tryon Park, with beautiful views of the
Hudson, the Washington Bridge, and the cliffs of New Jersey.*

Visit the Van Cortlandt House Museum in the Bronx and imagine the
daily life of a wealthy colonial family in the 18ᵗʰ century.

Many great luminaries from American history (including George Washington)
have passed through the doors of the Van Cortlandt House Museum, which
was built in 1748.

DEEP DIVE

THE NEW YORK CITY SUBWAY

After the introduction of a steam train service on Manhattan's principal routes, New York unveiled its first underground subway lines to an astonished public in 1904. The network that emerged would become one of the largest in the world.

With its Romanesque Revival arches, stained-glass windows, and chandeliers, the now-closed City Hall subway station offers a glimpse of the decor that awaited the passengers on the city's first underground line when it opened on 27 October 1904. It closed to traffic in 1945 but is sometimes still opened up by staff of the New York Transit Museum. The historic subway exits and entrances which have survived in the Manhattan cityscape show how important this new mode of transport was for New Yorkers.

The subway can often appear intimidating to the inexperienced, but it is the quickest and cheapest way of getting across the city's five boroughs from north to south and from east to west. It transports several million passengers each day on more than 248 miles (399 km) of track. Most of the train lines, which operate 24/7, run underground, especially in Manhattan. They are designated with letters and numbers that will help you to find your way as you enter stations or once inside.

The first step is to work out your intended direction of travel. There are generally separate entrances on either side of a street or avenue, with signs for Uptown (heading north across Manhattan toward Harlem and the Bronx) or Downtown (toward the Financial District and Brooklyn) to make things easier. Maps in the subway or electronic display panels on the platforms help you to navigate this giant maze, and these can often be more reliable than the signs on the car windows.

Station complexes such as those at Union Square or Times Square serve as interchanges between various lines, although it can sometimes be wise to limit transfers in large stations, even if it means walking longer at street level, in order to avoid having to navigate endless underground corridors, especially at rush hour. Another useful tip is to use local and express lines appropriately. Stations served by local trains are easily identified on a map by their black dots while express trains stop only at white dots. These are very popular with New Yorkers, as skipping numerous stops can save precious time. You should also be cautious about traveling at weekends, particularly to and from Brooklyn, as track maintenance work is frequently carried out then. Downloading the Metropolitan Transportation Authority (MTA) app to your cellphone will make it easier to keep up to date.

THE NEW YORK SUBWAY

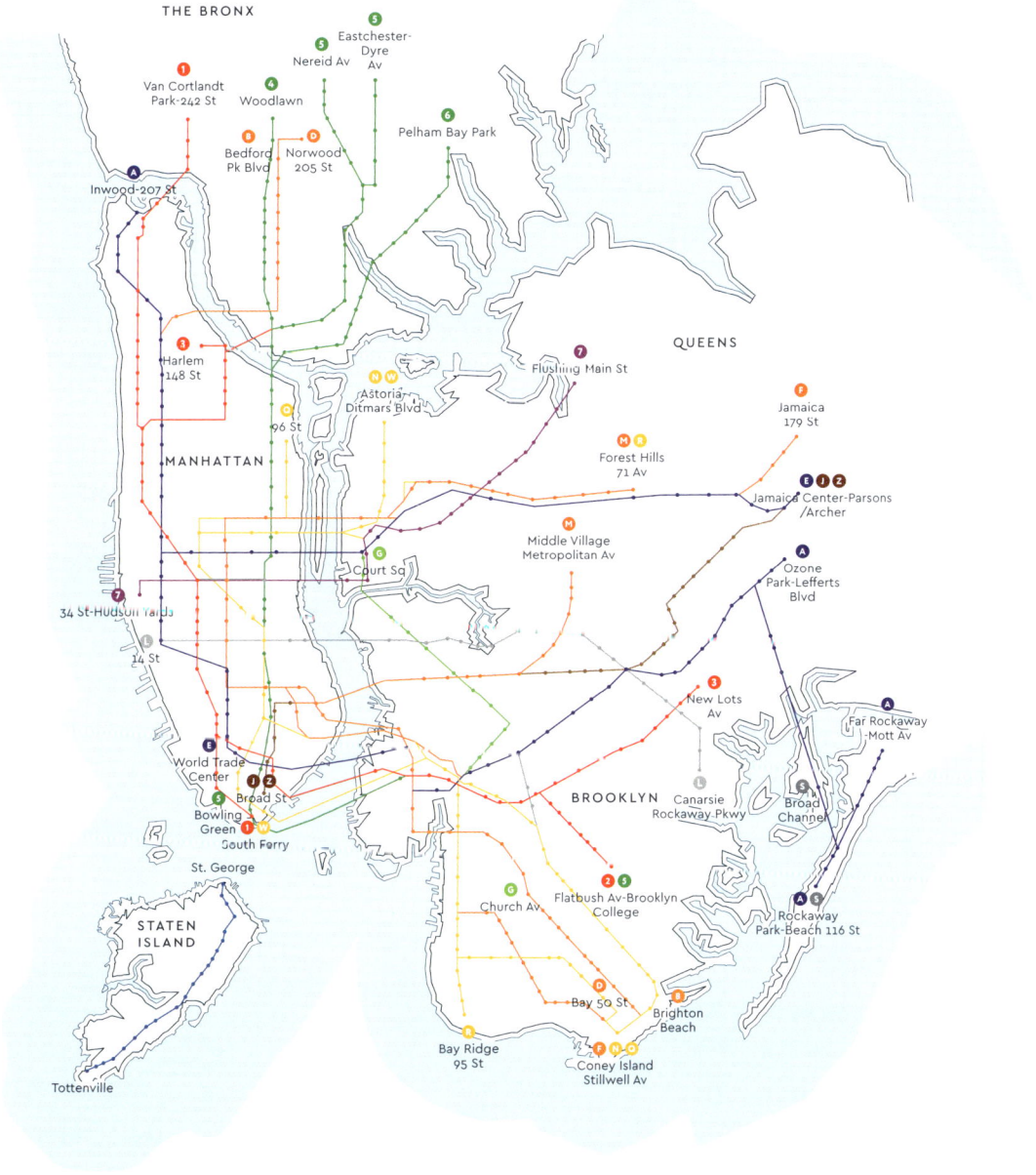

THE BRONX

Van Cortlandt
Park-242 St

Woodlawn

Nereid Av

Eastchester-
Dyre
Av

Pelham Bay Park

Bedford
Pk Blvd

Norwood
205 St

Inwood-207 St

Harlem
148 St

QUEENS

Flushing Main St

Astoria-
Ditmars Blvd

Jamaica
179 St

96 St

MANHATTAN

Forest Hills
71 Av

Jamaica Center-Parsons
/Archer

Middle Village
Metropolitan Av

Court Sq

Ozone
Park-Lefferts
Blvd

34 St-Hudson Yards

14 St

New Lots
Av

Far Rockaway
-Mott Av

World Trade
Center

Broad St

BROOKLYN

Canarsie
Rockaway Pkwy

Broad
Channel

Bowling
Green

South Ferry

St. George

Flatbush Av-Brooklyn
College

Rockaway
Park-Beach 116 St

STATEN
ISLAND

Church Av

Bay 50 St

Brighton
Beach

Bay Ridge
95 St

Coney Island
Stillwell Av

Tottenville

WEEKENDS				
B No service (use C, D, Q)	**M** Delancey St/ Essex St-Metropolitan Av	**6** Local in Manhattan, via Manhattan Bridge	**W** No service (use N, R)	**5** Dyre Av-Bowling Green

NIGHT SUBWAY (daily from midnight to 6am)						
A Local, 207 St- Far Rockaway. Euclid Av-Lefferts Blvd Shuttle	**C** No service (use A)	**E** Local service	**B** No service (use A, D, Q)	**D** Local in Brooklyn	**M** Myrtle Av-Metropolitan Av Shuttle	**S** No service (use 7)
N Local, via Financial District	**Q** Local service	**R** Whitehall St-95 St	**W** No service (use N)	**2** Local service	**3** 148 St-Times Sq/42 St	**4** Local, Woodlawn-New Lots Av Skips Hoyt St	**5** Dyre Av- E180 St Shuttle

LIFESTYLE

MOUNT MORRIS PARK HISTORIC DISTRICT

A RICH PAST

The elegant brownstones in this neighborhood named after an 18th-century
American senator earned it recognition as a Historic District of the city in 1971.

ICONIC

The Mount Morris Fire Watchtower was built in what is now Marcus Garvey Park in 1855 as a place to watch over Manhattan and prevent fires.

ICE CREAMS

The flavors at Sugar Hill Creamery (184 Lenox Avenue) take their inspiration from Harlem residents from the Caribbean and elsewhere.

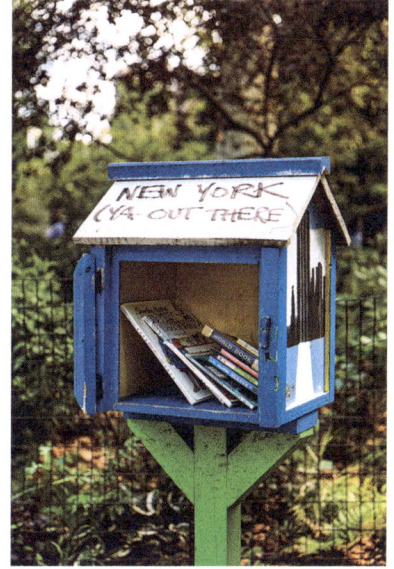

GRANDEUR

These buildings bear witness to the ambition of real estate developers at the end of the 19th century.

COMMUNITY

The park, named after Black nationalist Marcus Garvey, is full of life during the day.

GO GREEN

Plant Corner has a wide selection of plants for sale in what was once a private home at 183 Malcolm X Boulevard.

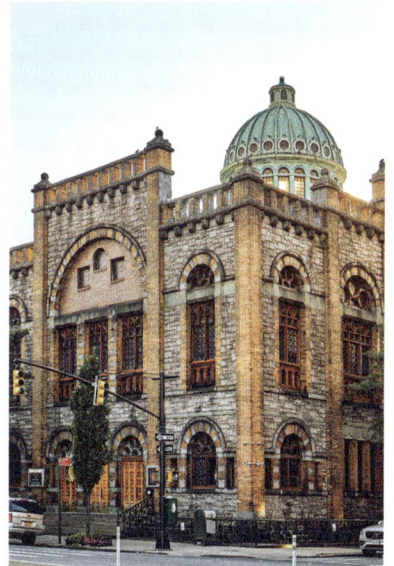

HELP YOURSELF

Passers-by can choose a book to read on a bench from a mini library.

PLACE OF WORSHIP

Mount Morris Ascension Presbyterian Church was built of granite and gold Roman brick.

ABOVE

Wave Hill is a lovely place to visit on a beautiful summer's afternoon.

OPPOSITE

You will find tropical flowers, cacti, and other succulents in the Marco Polo
Stufano Conservatory.

ABOVE

*The fresco designed by Louis Delsarte (2005) opposite the Apollo Theater
celebrates the creative spirit at work in Harlem between the wars.*

OPPOSITE

*This house designed by the architect James Brown Lord at the end of the
19th century is one of the prized homes on Strivers' Row.*

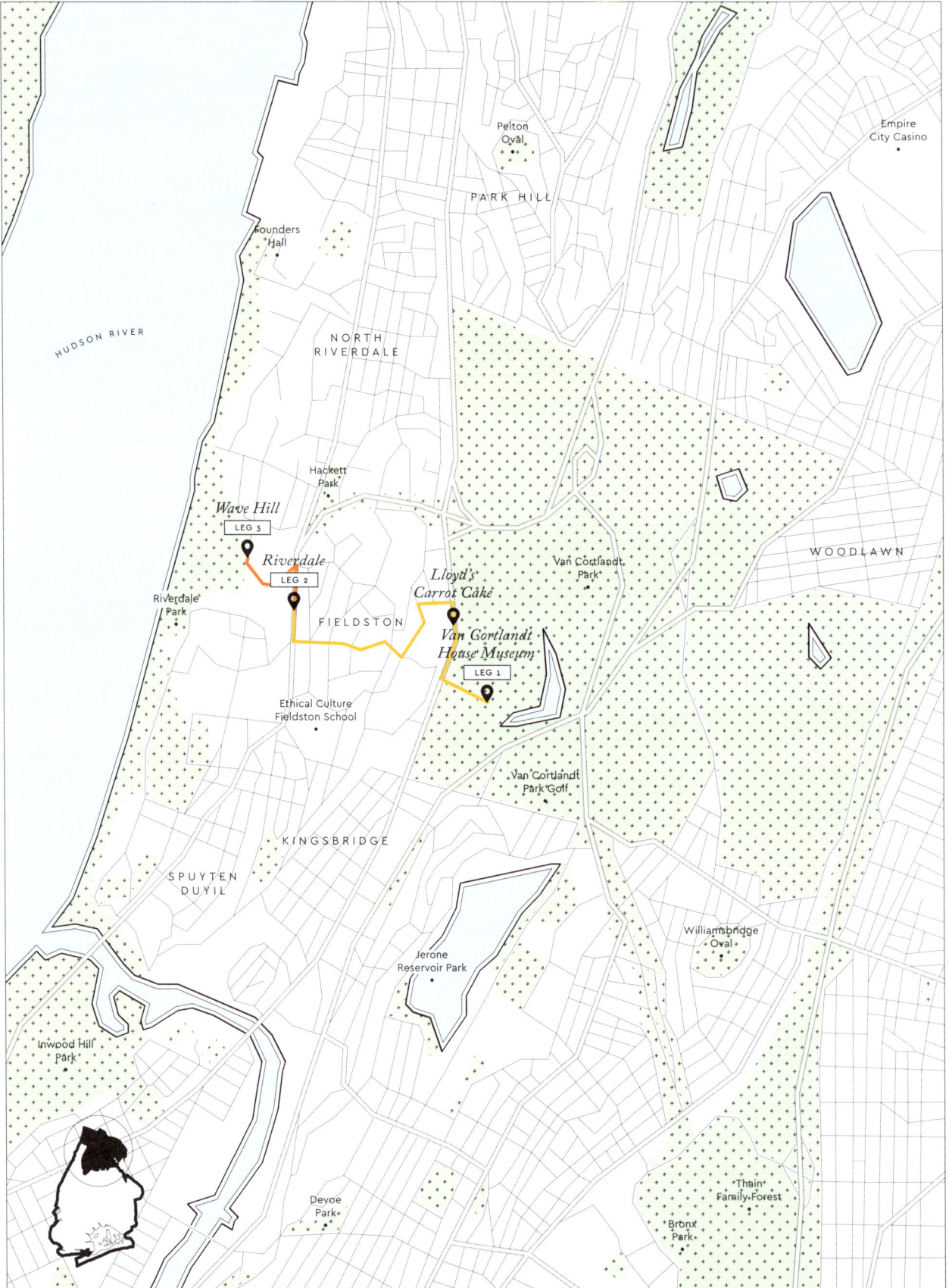

HUDSON RIVER

Empire
City Casino

Pelton
Oval

PARK HILL

Founders
Hall

NORTH
RIVERDALE

WOODLAWN

Hackett
Park

Wave Hill
LEG 3

Riverdale
LEG 2

Lloyd's
Carrot Cake

Van Cortlandt
Park

Riverdale
Park

FIELDSTON

Van Cortlandt
House Museum
LEG 1

Ethical Culture
Fieldston School

Van Cortlandt
Park Golf

KINGSBRIDGE

SPUYTEN
DUYIL

Williamsbridge
Oval

Jerone
Reservoir Park

Inwood Hill
Park

Thain
Family Forest

Devoe
Park

Bronx
Park

THE GARDENS OF THE BRONX

After the concrete jungle of Manhattan, the Bronx offers a bucolic retreat for nature lovers, with leafy residential neighborhoods, parks, and woods that attract strollers in search of some peace and quiet.

LEG 1 : VAN CORTLANDT HOUSE MUSEUM

This house made of carved stone tucked away in Van Cortlandt Park is a witness to an age when the wealthy amassed empires through the sweat of their slaves. The mansion, the oldest in the Bronx, was built as a home by Dutch grain merchant Frederick Van Cortlandt in 1748. The surrounding plantations have been replaced by large green spaces that are now enjoyed by local families and sports fans. The residence, which is run as one of the City of New York's historic house museums, is open to the public from Wednesday to Sunday. Conservation work has restored the interior to very close to its original state, and visitors can clearly imagine how life must once have been lived. George Washington spent time here in 1776 and 1783 during the American Revolutionary War.

LEG 2 : RIVERDALE

Stop off at Lloyd's (6087 Broadway) to buy a slice of carrot cake and then head to Riverdale, a well-to-do neighborhood in the northern reaches of the Bronx. Turn left at the corner of W 251st Street and sneak through the parking lot between the buildings to your left to reach Tibbett Avenue and begin your climb into the pretty neighborhood of Fieldston. The winding, rocky paths will take you past rows of elegant residences, some of which resemble medieval castles. A wealthy local family commissioned one of the creators of Central Park to develop this enclave where the centuries-old trees are often looked after by private tree surgeons. The road that runs along beneath the path leads to Riverdale, an equally charming neighborhood of old farms with pastel shutters, stone mansions, and timber-clad homes. It was in this very tranquil setting beside the Hudson that one John Fitzgerald Kennedy grew up, at 5040 Independence Avenue.

LEG 3 : WAVE HILL

Pass by the homes and flowerbeds of Riverdale to reach this 27-acre (11-ha) estate, one of New York City's hidden paradises. It can be explored from the country house built beside the Hudson by a wealthy family in 1843 whose subsequent occupants include Theodore Roosevelt and Mark Twain. A greenhouse and various kinds of vegetation can be found in the English-style garden, but what makes this area unique are the views across the Hudson valley. The stone benches installed at vantage points add to the Romanticism of this unexpected stolen moment in your exploration of Manhattan.

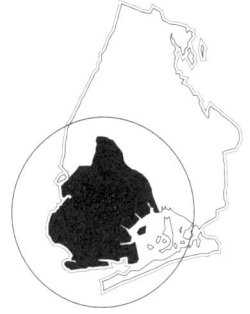

BROOKLYN

A bridge has connected the former Dutch village of Brooklyn to Manhattan since 1883. New York's most populous borough is multi-faceted thanks to its architecture, a hotch-potch that reflects its industrial and residential heritage. Many families and artists who enjoy its gentler pace of life have made their homes here.

P.196

*The colorful facade of the florist Stems Brooklyn blends in perfectly in the
Bushwick neighborhood, famous for its murals.*

OPPOSITE

*Enjoy a breathtaking view of the East River and the bridges linking Brooklyn and Manhattan
from this beach in the heart of Main Street Park under Manhattan Bridge.*

The days when Brooklyn equaled boring are long gone. Ever since the 1990s and the
television series *Sex and the City* (in which a move to this vast borough immediately
entailed a life of relentless tedium), its residents have been eager to sweep such
clichés aside. It is now impossible to ignore these beautiful neighborhoods with their
rows of brownstones and the docks along the East River that exude authenticity.

It is worth saving some time for this former Dutch colony, founded in the 17th century,
whose name may be derived from *breuckelen* ("broken earth"). It is divided up into
a long patchwork of neighborhoods that feel very different thanks to the many
different communities living there. It is also here that artists tired of Manhattan
rents have migrated, along with families in search of a slower pace of life. The
neighborhood of Brooklyn Heights was built across from Lower Manhattan and
enjoys unmatched views of the skyline of the southern tip of the island. A host of
actors and authors have also taken up residence in its elegant red sandstone houses.
Downtown Brooklyn is just a stroll away and from there you can explore the old
Navy Yard with its factories and creative studios.

Williamsburg has polished up the rather wild image that has long clung to its streets,
and indeed has gone too far, according to some who deplore its gentrification. It is
still a pleasant place to visit, with its old wooden houses, cafés, bookstores, bodegas,
and boutiques selling the work of local artisans. Nearby Greenpoint is a great
place to immerse yourself in local life beside the water before trying one of its
excellent restaurants.

Propelled by a feverish real estate market, Williamsburg's artists have headed to Red
Hook and Bushwick, which, crammed in between a couple of workshops or
warehouses, still retain the image of Brooklyn of yesteryear. You will find gleaming
icons of old America, impressive murals, and boutiques with a dizzying selection of
vintage fashion, from jeans to cowboy boots. It has a very particular American feel.

After visiting the Botanic Garden or the Brooklyn Museum, don't miss the
residential neighborhood of Park Slope to the west of Prospect Park, with its tranquil
streets lined with magnificent brownstones. From here, simply hop onto the subway
and take the Q line to the final station at Coney Island to bathe in nostalgia, and
enjoy its old-world amusement park and oceanfront beach. This very different and
unexpected atmosphere is a reminder that New York is a city surrounded by water.

THE ESSENTIALS

48

BROOKLYN BOTANIC GARDEN

This 52-acre (21-ha) botanic garden opened its gates in 1910 and is noted in particular for its Japanese garden, which is one of the oldest in the country.

49

FORT GREENE FARMERS MARKET

Local growers assemble every Saturday to sell seasonal fruit and veg (amongst other things) and promote local delivery channels.

50

BROOKLYN BRIDGE

This suspension bridge was opened in 1883 to link Manhattan and Brooklyn across the East River.

51

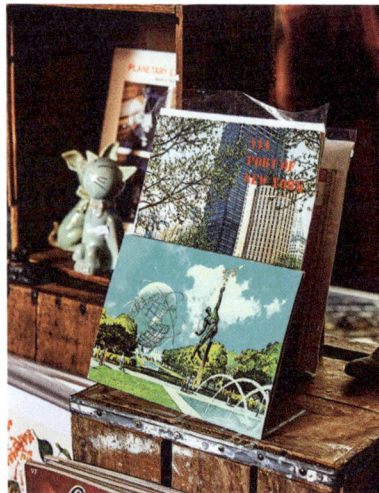

BROOKLYN FLEA MARKET

This flea market opened in 2008 sells antiques, vintage furniture, designer clothes, and beautifully made craft objects.

52

CONEY ISLAND

A seaside neighborhood in southern Brooklyn that is famous for its beaches, promenade, and amusement parks, such as Luna Park.

53

PARK SLOPE

A residential Brooklyn neighborhood noted for its beautiful 19th-century brownstones, highly reputed schools, and family feel.

54

GRAND ARMY PLAZA

This square was laid out in 1895 around the Soldiers' and Sailors' Memorial Arch commemorating those who fought in the American Civil War.

55

BROOKLYN PUBLIC LIBRARY

An Art Deco building completed in 1941 that holds more than a million volumes.

56

BROOKLYN HEIGHTS PROMENADE

A promenade laid out in the 1950s that offers panoramic views of the Manhattan skyline, the East River, and the Statue of Liberty.

57

MONTAGUE STREET

This shopping street is the main drag of Brooklyn Heights and is noted for its restaurants, cafés, and boutiques.

58

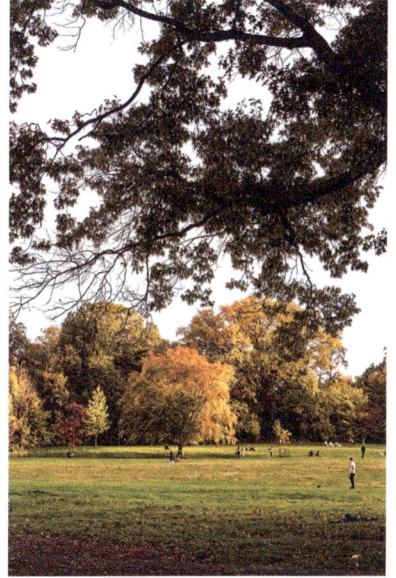

PROSPECT PARK

This park was designed by Frederick Law Olmsted and Calvert Vaux, the architects of Central Park, and opened in 1867. It is the largest in Brooklyn, with an area of 526 acres (213 ha).

59

BROOKLYN MUSEUM

Since opening in 1895, this museum (the third largest in New York) has acquired holdings of more than 560,000 exhibits and is known for its vast collection of Ancient Egyptian art.

ABOVE

The muted lighting and patinated walls of the Achilles Heel bar
in Greenpoint have a unique charm.

OPPOSITE

Williamsburg's stores resolutely nurture the bohemian spirit
that has made the neighborhood such a success.

ABOVE

*The discreet entrance to Maison Premiere in Williamsburg is
reminiscent of the timeless elegance of bars in New Orleans.*

OPPOSITE

*The old Domino Sugar Refinery in Williamsburg is a witness
to the neighborhood's industrial past.*

The metal span of Williamsburg Bridge is silhouetted against the skyline as One World Trade Center looms in the distance.

PORTRAIT

ON THE WATERFRONT

TAYLOR PATTERSON

Floral designer Taylor Patterson has created a space a mere
stone's throw from the East River and the Williamsburg Bridge
to showcase her passion for plant species of every kind.

Fox Fodder Farm, the floral design studio founded by Taylor Patterson in 2011, overlooks a back courtyard paved with bluestone designed by the landscape architect Brook Klausing. "I wanted to create a flower store like the one I dreamed of visiting, an environment like a haven where you could find peace," she explains – and this is precisely what greets those who are in no hurry to leave when they come to pick out a bouquet or take a moment out of their daily tasks.

In a way, Taylor has been trying to recreate on the Brooklyn waterfront the rural Delaware surroundings in which she grew up. After a lifetime in New York City, she has put down roots here and travels up every week to spend a few days with her team in a street just off the vibrant center of Williamsburg. "When I settled in New York, I missed nature and the meaning it brings; flowers can teach us so much, starting with patience and resilience."

Taylor, who studied History of Art, has had a career in several parts that has also been influenced by the years she spent in Paris, during which she worked with a landscape gardener, absorbing all kinds of inspirations. It was Marc Chagall, André Derain, and a whole roster of other artists whose work she came across in museums who taught her mastery of color. "In Paris, I would see florists on every street corner. Unlike in New York City, flowers are part of the culture there." Taylor began to enjoy creating her own flower arrangements and, just a few years later, a wedding for which she designed the floral displays was featured in *Vogue*, and this lent her wings. The studio's clientele now includes fashion houses, lifestyle brands, restaurants, bars, and stylists who are taking an increasing interest in bringing the natural world into urban settings.

Venture inside to catch Taylor or one of her teammates in the process of arranging bouquets that are often a little on the wild side; "I love to let flowers express themselves, and I accept a certain imperfection in my compositions that imparts a unique aesthetic." Passing visitors may also chance upon one or two vases made by local artisans. "I invite those who come here to appreciate flowers as much as I do. To my mind, a single stem is enough to create a very beautiful effect if it is arranged in the right vase," she points out. Her favorites are daffodils, the flowers of her childhood on the family farm, and she loves to combine these and other, mostly local, varieties with branches collected at the end of winter in New York City.

Taylor Patterson works with her team to create
bouquets of flowers with a rustic feel.

INSPIRATION

You will always come away from a visit to
Fox Fodder Farm with new ideas for your home.

Creativity is a family business at Stems Brooklyn in Bushwick,
as Donut, the flower workshop mascot, ably proves.

Color is king in the old speakeasy where Suzanna Cameron opened her store in
2013, a flower bar where bouquets from a vast array of flowers are made.

BOHEMIAN BUSHWICK

LA CANTINE

Ioana Hercberg has opened a luncheonette inspired by American diners and French cafés
in an old grocery store on the corner of Saint Nicholas Avenue and Willoughby Avenue.

FINE AND RAW

This chocolate makers at 70 Scott Avenue specializes in bean-to-bar chocolate.

STEMS BROOKLYN

An old speakeasy at 96 Knickerbocker Avenue has been converted into a florist.

ROBERTA'S

Food lovers flock to 261 Moore Street for the pizzas and the quiet of its courtyard.

KNICKERBOCKER AVENUE

Murals and nice places to eat await discovery in this street.

L TRAIN VINTAGE

The place to come for jeans, cowboy boots, and t-shirts. You can shop for a complete American outfit at 1377 DeKalb Avenue.

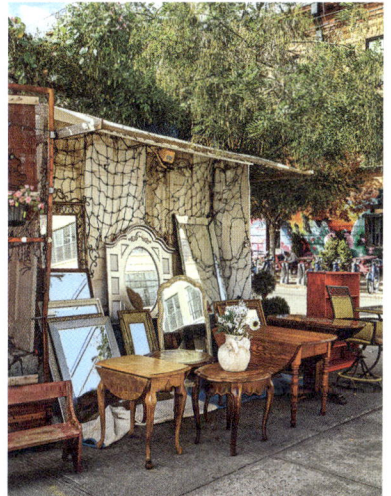

HENRY'S

This liquor store at 69 Central Avenue stocks a wide selection of natural wines.

AMERICAN VINTAGE

Come and check out the vintage cars, like this 1940s Chevy.

FLEA MARKET

Pick up some vintage furniture on the sidewalk.

MURALS

An artists' collective has decorated the walls at the corner of Saint Nicholas Avenue and Jefferson Street.

It's worth waiting in line outside for the delicious ice creams served at the Brooklyn Ice Cream Factory in Dumbo (an acronym for Down Under the Manhattan Bridge Overpass).

The iconic span of the Manhattan Bridge (a favorite subject for tourist snaps of New York) can be seen from the streets of Dumbo.

DEEP DIVE

THE BROWNSTONES

Brownstones are houses of red, pink or chestnut-brown sandstone
that began to appear in the 19th century and they are an integral part
of New York's popular image. Their elegant lines hark back to
a time when life was very different.

With their majestic stone stoops, high windows, and oriels jutting out into the street, brownstones are a distinctive feature of the New York cityscape. Families who could afford the privilege in the 1800s were obsessed with moving up in the world both figuratively and literally. The often unpaved streets were frequented by horses and carts that would leave behind evidence of their presence, much to local chagrin. A sitting room and dining room away from the filth, odor, and noise made daily life far more agreeable.

Brownstone is actually a sandstone, rich in the iron oxide that gives it a hue ranging from red to chestnut-brown, and is mainly quarried in New Jersey and Connecticut. The rock, which was less expensive than limestone and marble, allowed the middle classes to afford sophisticated facades as it could be used to face a brick structure. The idea behind these new townhouses had been inspired by the blocks of terraced homes that had been spreading through British cities since the 16th century. The interior was arranged over three to five floors and would include a high-ceilinged reception area decorated with moldings, wood paneling, chimney breasts, and sometimes even marble columns. The basement was usually reserved for the servants who saw to the comfort of their lords and masters.

Such homes lent themselves nicely to adaptation according to the imagination, or indeed pretensions, of their owners, and a range of styles flourished, from Queen Anne to Greek or Gothic Revival, adorned with remarkable frills and furbelows thanks to the skill of local craftsmen. As time progressed, the brownstones would provide a pleasant contrast to the austerity of modern New York architecture as it progressed skyward. While you will also come across brownstones in Manhattan and Harlem, the finest examples are to be admired in Brooklyn, in particular in the neighborhood of Brooklyn Heights, the first residential suburb of New York, which was laid out during the 1820s, and in Park Slope overlooking Prospect Park, a popular leisure spot for the city's middle classes. It was the old-world charm of these houses that has been tempting many young Manhattan families to up sticks to Brooklyn since the 1980s. When the real estate market exploded in the 2000s, many single-family houses were divided into multiple apartments and these highly prized homes are now beyond the purses of many New Yorkers. Architects and designers take on the delicate task of remodeling them to preserve their highly valuable artistic heritage while incorporating the amenities demanded by their modern owners. Every floor of a brownstone is now used to its full potential.

ARCHITECTURAL STYLES OF BROWNSTONES

FEDERAL

GREEK REVIVAL

ITALIAN

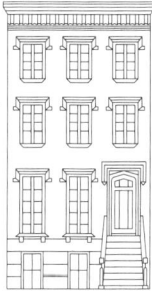

GOTHIC REVIVAL

NEOCLASSICAL REVIVAL

SECOND EMPIRE

QUEEN ANNE

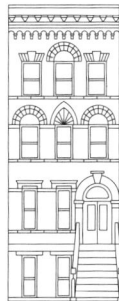

ROMANESQUE REVIVAL

RENAISSANCE REVIVAL

A HOST OF STYLES

Brownstones are a very recognizable part of New York's popular image
and Brooklyn and Harlem are home to the greatest variety.

ABOVE

*The Jewish community has been established in Brooklyn Heights since the
1960s, settling around synagogues, yeshivas, and kosher businesses.*

OPPOSITE

*Stroll along the East River Esplanade and admire the buildings in the
very peaceful neighborhood of Brooklyn Heights.*

ABOVE

Many of the streets in Brooklyn Heights are lined with brownstones that were mainly built in the 19th century.

OPPOSITE

The lawns of Brooklyn Botanic Garden are a riot of bluebells in spring.

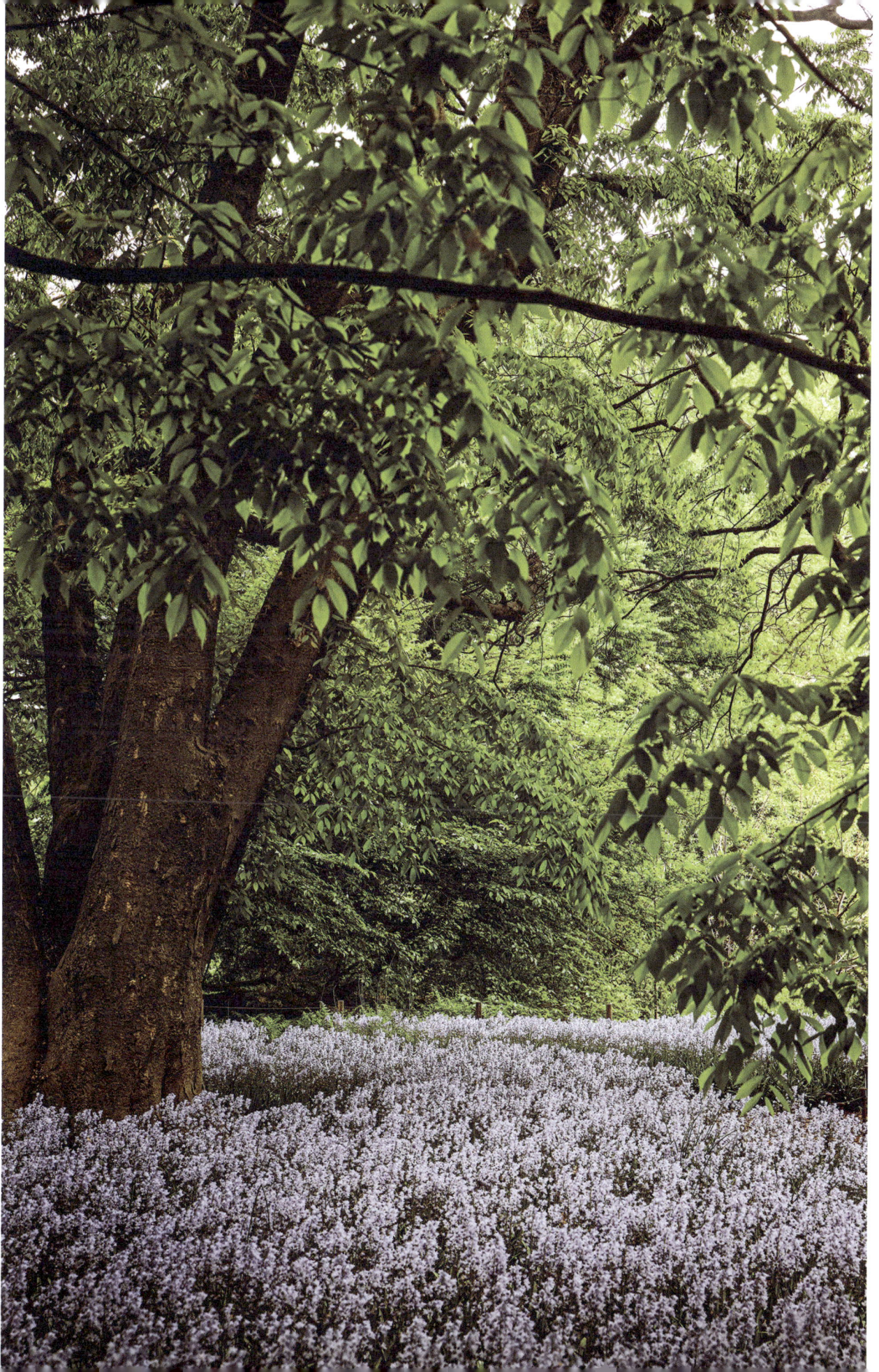

PORTRAIT

THE BEAUTY OF A GESTURE

YOONA HUR

Korean-born artist Yoona Hur weaves tradition and modernity in her work,
which she creates from clay and paper in a studio in the creative hub of Industry City
in Sunset Park.

Yoona Hur left Korea for North America with her parents at the age of twelve, but visitors to her studio are invariably greeted with rituals that are closely linked to her homeland. You are invited to remove your shoes at the entrance and put on slippers, a whiff of incense floats in the air, and the hostess makes tea. "I love to create an atmosphere around my creations, to go a step further. These rituals are an integral part of practicing my art," she emphasizes.

In 2023, the artist, whose vases and sculptures have been exhibited at Amelie, Maison d'Art and at Galerie Was in Manhattan, moved into a workspace in Industry City, a large complex in the Sunset Park neighborhood that is home to many creative artists. Yoona painted her bright and airy space white and her pieces encouraged new perspectives through their subtle juxtaposition of shapes and materials.

The former New York architect is also a graduate of the Art Institute of Chicago, but she came to clay after six years of intense work in a field that was too abstract for her taste. Eager to reconnect with the material, she took weekend ceramics classes and treated herself to a long stay in the land of her ancestors. Her experiences with Korean antiquities held in the Metropolitan Museum of Art were also

a turning point in her artistic journey. "After settling in New York in 2006 to study architecture, I got into the habit of visiting the museum to seek inspiration and peace. When I discovered the Moon Jar from the Joseon period (1392-1910) in the Korean gallery, the simplicity, spirituality, and timelessness it embodied really spoke to me and helped me to reconnect with my roots," she recounts.

Her studio looks out into the sky, and the artist spends her days creating a dialogue between the past and the present. The lines of her repertoire of shapes echo Korean antiques and borrow from the nature she observes in her urban refuges, from the community gardens of the West Village to the green hills of the Bronx and the flower markets where she likes to lose herself at weekends. Her *Wild Garden* collection of sculptures was inspired by birds, clouds, and flowers. "With the collection, I am striving to explore the whole concept of a garden, a bit like a gardener who sows a seed and watches as the plant grows from it or, more broadly, as life develops in harmony with the seasons and unexpected elements." Through her work in clay and more recently with *hanji* (traditional Korean paper made with mulberry bark), Yoona has in essence embarked on a quest for balance, an essential quality in a city in constant flux like the one in which she has made her home.

The artist's sculptures often incorporate shapes
inspired by nature.

ARRANGEMENTS

Yoona's creative process involves installing her
works in her light-filled studio.

ABOVE

*No visit to Coney Island is complete without a hot dog from the
kiosk at Nathan's, a New York institution.*

OPPOSITE

*The Parachute Jump originated at the 1939 New York World's Fair
and looks out over the Coney Island boardwalk.*

GREENWICH
VILLAGE

Union
Square

GRAMERCY
PARK

GREENPOINT

Washington
Square Park

SOHO

East
Village

EAST RIVER

Bushwick
Inlet Park

LOWER
MANHATTAN

Tenement
Museum

CHINATOWN

Two
Bridges

Corlears
Hook Park

Williamsburg
Bridge

WILLIAMBURG

Manhattan
Bridge

Brooklyn
Bridge

Dumbo

LEG 2

Vinegar Hill

LEG 1

SOUTH
WILLIAMBURG

Brooklyn
Storehouse

Brooklyn
Bridge Park

Brooklyn
Heights

LEG 3

Truman
Capote's House

Brooklyn
Navy Yard

Brooklyn
Bridge Park

Commodore
Barry Park

DOWNTOWN
BROOKLYN

ALL ALONG THE LOWER MANHATTAN SKYLINE

Flowing beneath the Manhattan Bridge, the East River passes industrial buildings,
art galleries, and gardens on its journey toward Brooklyn Heights.
There are magnificent views of the skyscrapers of Lower Manhattan
from this tranquil neighborhood of brownstone-lined streets.

LEG 1 : VINEGAR HILL

Vinegar Hill stands between the old Brooklyn Navy Yard and the Manhattan Bridge as a memento of New York's rich industrial past. Exploring this quiet corner (the name of which derives from a 1798 battle in Ireland) will whisk you away from the tourists to a location of warehouses, old factories, and architecture that blends the legacy of the past with the aspirations of modern realtors. The high ground of this neighborhood, where Irish immigrants settled at the turn of the 19th century, features buildings built on roads paved with what are known as Belgian blocks, a reference to the porphyry or sandstone used as ballast on boats bound for New York from Antwerp in the 14th century. A brief foray onto its streets, with a distinctly European charm in places, provides an interesting perspective on the urban development of Brooklyn's waterfront and surroundings.

LEG 2 : DUMBO

With its lavishly renovated old industrial buildings and five-star views of Lower Manhattan, Dumbo (an acronym for Down Under the Manhattan Bridge Overpass) has become a magnet for wealthy young New Yorkers, much to the disgruntlement of the artists who helped its rebirth during the 1980s. Its cobbled streets lead you past art and design galleries, but the real draw is Brooklyn Bridge Park. Don't miss Jane's Carousel, an old merry-go-round restored by the artist Jane Walentas that has been installed in an acrylic pavilion designed by architect Jean Nouvel. Not far away, try a lobster roll from Luke's Lobster kiosk and follow it up with an ice cream from the Brooklyn Ice Cream Factory just down the street. The old industrial area has been turned into green spaces and a beach and is a perfect spot in which to lie down on the grass and enjoy the pace of waterfront life.

LEG 3 : BROOKLYN HEIGHTS

Squibb Park Bridge is a zig-zagging walkway built between Brooklyn Bridge Park and Squibb Park by Pier 1 to provide access to the charming residential neighborhood of Brooklyn Heights, the first suburb established in the United States at the turn of the 19th century. The brownstones here are amongst the most beautiful in Brooklyn and definitely worth a detour. You will still find a few tastefully restored wooden houses and, although many individual homes have been divided up into apartments, there is a definite grandeur to the place. Try to include Truman Capote's house in your itinerary but the ideal approach is to bounce between the majestic red sandstone houses and the old stables that have been converted into apartments at the end of cul-de-sacs. Enjoy a moment at the end of your stroll (preferably during the so-called golden hour) to admire the views of the East River and the Lower Manhattan skyline.

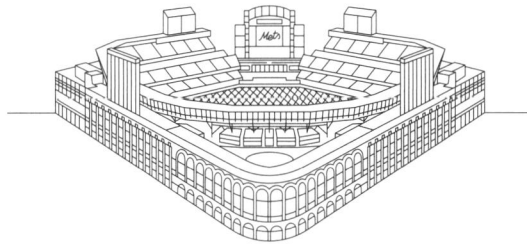

QUEENS

This borough named after Catherine of Braganza, the wife of English king Charles II, has become the largest in New York City. It is also where you will encounter the greatest number of foreign cultures, thanks to the generations of immigrants who have been putting down roots here since the turn of the 20th century. It is here too that ocean is visible at the end of a street of suburban houses.

P.228

*Owners of the timber-clad houses in The Belle Harbor neighborhood
on the Rockaway Peninsula enjoy a tranquil life beside the sea.*

OPPOSITE

*The elevated subway affords magnificent views of the neighborhood
and the Manhattan skyline as it crosses Queens.*

The New York World's Fair lit up the city in 1964 from its Flushing Meadows-Corona Park site in Queens, and you will still find the occasional souvenir of the celebrations in some local flea markets. There is also an enormous metal globe to commemorate the event, a fitting symbol of a borough whose residents come from around the globe and where more than 180 languages are spoken. The area was colonized by the Dutch in 1642 but only really began to fill up with people with the construction of the Queensboro Bridge and an elevated subway line at the turn of the 20th century, allowing immigrants crammed into the tenements of Lower Manhattan to find more comfortable quarters. The 7 Flushing Local and Express services connect Times Square and Flushing above ground over about ten miles (16 km), passing through neighborhoods where many communities have settled, earning the line the popular nickname of the International Express. A trip through the neighborhoods of Astoria, Flushing, and Jackson Heights will give you a taste of Greek, Chinese, and Indian cuisine.

New York's febrile real estate market continues to lure Manhattan and Brooklyn families to Queens. The atmosphere in Ridgewood, in the south of the borough, is reminiscent of that in the adjacent neighborhood of Bushwick in Brooklyn, where many artists settled in the 2010s. Linger for a while amongst the luncheonettes and charming retro grocery stores on these quiet streets. Long Island City in the far west by Hunter's Point on the banks of the East River shows a very different and resolutely modern face, designed to attract a younger clientele. Gantry Plaza State Park, which opened in 1998 amongst modern buildings and old warehouses, offers a succession of gardens, lawns, and skateparks, but the views across to the Midtown skyline in Manhattan make it worth the detour.

The artist Isamu Noguchi chose to settle in Long Island City, tucked away in a corner of Astoria, in the 1960s, and went on to create a museum-garden that remains open to this day, while the Socrates Sculpture Park, not far away, is a place for the young and the talented to exhibit their work in the open air. Although Queens is New York City's second-most populous borough, nature is never far away, and this residential neighborhood feels like England with its cottages surrounded by flower gardens. Some distance away, Rockaway Beach looks out over the Atlantic, and this wild strand is popular with surfers when the weather is warm. Here, as elsewhere in this metropolis, the change of scenery is an integral part of the journey.

THE ESSENTIALS

60

HUNTER'S POINT SOUTH WATERFRONT PARK

There are beautiful views of the Manhattan skyline from this park,
along with cycle paths and playgrounds.

61

CITI FIELD

The New York Mets' 41,922-seater stadium opened in 2009. Look out for the Home Run Apple, the club's victory symbol.

62

THE LOUIS ARMSTRONG HOUSE

The famous jazz musician's house has become a museum dedicated to his work and life.

63

MOMA PS1

This contemporary art center has acquired a reputation for immersive exhibitions, in situ installations, and a program of artistic residences.

64

SOCRATES SCULPTURE PARK

This open-air exhibition space built on an old industrial site in 1986 is dedicated to contemporary art, with a notable display of monumental sculptures.

65

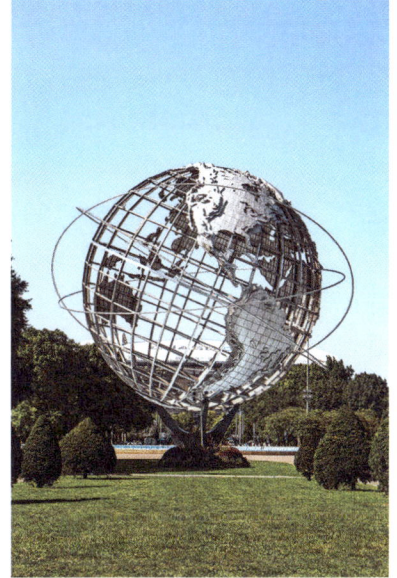

FLUSHING MEADOWS-CORONA PARK

Queens' largest park hosted the World's Fairs of 1939 and 1964, and contemporary features such as the Unisphere and the New York State Pavilion have been preserved.

66

RIDGEWOOD

This neighborhood on the borders of Brooklyn is noted for the preserved architecture of its brick row houses.

ABOVE

*The old-world decor, flavorful sandwiches, and friendly service at
Salty Lunch Lady's Little Luncheonette in Ridgewood will tempt food lovers.*

OPPOSITE

*A vintage Fiat convertible awaits new adventures
in a residential street in Queens.*

NATURE

ROCKAWAY BEACH

LOW SEASON

Enjoy the delightfully retro charm of a stroll along
Rockaway Beach on a beautiful day in the fall.

FORT TILDEN

Check out a landscape of dunes colonized by rugged vegetation from this old artillery fort.

RIGHT ON TIME

This 1891 clock was reinstalled beside the sea in Jacob Riis Park in 2019.

DUNES

Sea breezes trace sinuous lines in the white sand.

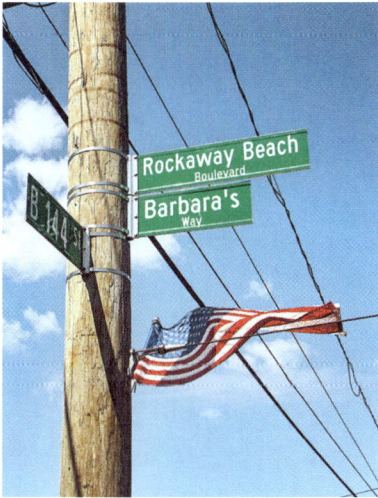

THE SUBURBS

You can see the ocean at the end of this suburban street over which American flags fly high.

SHADES

The streets of Rockaway are a riot of pretty colors once the summer season is over.

SEA AIR

The facades of houses near the beach are treated to protect them from the harsh, salty air.

PAVILIONS

Houses painted in pastel shades blend into the coastal scenery.

CALM

The vast expanses of sand can be enjoyed by locals when the holiday swimmers have gone home.

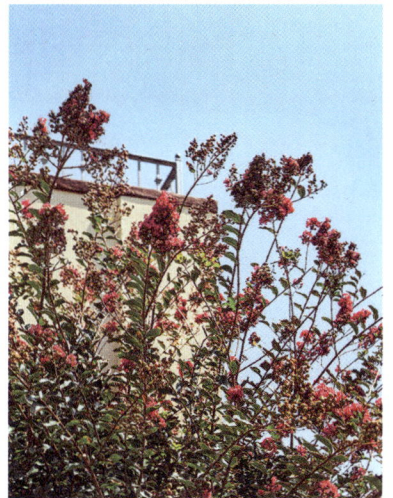

GARDENS

Shrubs and bushes are just part of the beauty of this seaside resort.

ABOVE

*As in Brooklyn, ice cream trucks make periodic appearances in the lives
of Queens residents on sunny days.*

OPPOSITE

*New York City's largest Indian, Pakistani, and Bangladeshi community
lives in Jackson Heights.*

There are impressive views of the Midtown skyline from the platforms of Queensboro Plaza subway station.

ABOVE

Colorful shingle facades with awnings alternate with brick buildings along the residential streets of Astoria.

OPPOSITE

Leo's Latticini, an Italian grocery store in Corona, known as Mama's to its regulars, has been dishing up generous panini with home-made mozzarella since 1935.

THE NOGUCHI MUSEUM

Toward the end of his life, the Japanese-born American artist Isamu Noguchi opened
a museum-garden in which New Yorkers could enjoy his abstract sculptures. The serenity
of this space continues to enchant visitors and inspire artists from
around the world.

In 1974, Isamu Noguchi bought an old photogravure plant opposite the building in Long Island City, Queens, in which he had set up his workshop thirteen years previously, far from the artistic bubble of Manhattan. He transferred some of his works to this new space and, when the gas station next door was put up for sale in 1980, he bought and demolished it, and, with the aid of architect Shoji Sadao, built a structure with a breeze-block facade. Over the next decade, he set about designing his most personal work, a museum that is home to more than two hundred of his creations, becoming the first artist in New York to realize such a dream.

The Isamu Noguchi Garden Museum threw open its doors in 1985, three years before the death of its creator. There is no clue from the street as to what awaits visitors to the building's 23,700 square feet (2,200 m²) of floorspace. The concrete pavilion houses the museum entrance and a gallery of stone sculptures resembling modern totems. The garden features more works amid a sea of green designed by the artist to encourage contemplation. This leads on to the old plant, whose girders and wooden beams have retained their original industrial charm and make the first encounter with the mysterious lines and fine materials (marble, granite, bronze, and brass) of the sculptures on the first floor all the more impressive.

The young Isamu Noguchi was heavily influenced by the modern approach to sculpture adopted by Constantin Brancusi, whose Parisian workshop he joined in 1927 to begin his first apprenticeship at the age of twenty-three. Here, the young artist, the son of a New York writer and a Japanese poet, was able to explore a wide range of abstract shapes with great sensitivity, and his numerous other trips overseas, in particular to Greece, Italy, Mexico, and Japan, would open up new horizons throughout his career.

A preference for unfussy shapes led Isamu Noguchi to an interest in furniture design, which he pursued with great success, and his wood and glass coffee tables have become some of the most iconic objects in contemporary design, along with his Akari collection of lamps crafted from *washi* (paper made from mulberry bark). These airborne sculptures inspired by traditional Asian lanterns have been made in Gifu in Japan since 1951 and now illuminate interiors around the world. As their designer has pointed out: "To make a home for yourself, all you need is a room, a tatami mat, and an Akari." There are plenty of different models to admire in the gift shop and even take home with you. These folding, featherweight lamps acquire a beautiful patina over time and are suitable for any living space.

1/ FROM THE SOURCE

The garden encourages a moment of contemplation with its
organically shaped sculptures and meticulously arranged plants.

2/ LANTERNS

A large selection of paper Akari
lamps are for sale in the store.

3/ SCULPTURES

The old studio is full of
sculptures in fine materials.

4/ TOTEMS

The entrance to the concrete pavilion
is filled with stone artworks.

WORLD LANGUAGES

The nationalities that rub shoulders in New York City on a daily basis help to make it a place of enormous cultural richness. While English and Spanish are the most common languages, you will hear many others spoken on the street.

A New York Times report of February 22, 2024 refers to a study carried out by linguists Ross Perlin and Daniel Kaufman on endangered languages spoken in various neighborhoods across the city. In the course of their research, they identified more than seven hundred languages in use, at least a hundred and fifty of which were in danger of dying out. The researchers recorded, transcribed, and translated the words of the people they interviewed, and went on to draft dictionaries and grammars for some of the languages they encountered. With residents from every corner of the planet, New York City is the best place to monitor this precious intangible cultural heritage.

Immigration has always played a key role in New York society. The original Dutch colonists were soon followed by British and French settlers and their African slaves, and the New World also welcomed inbound Irish, Germans, Italians, and Jews. Since then, refugees have continued to flock to a place where any dream seemed possible, and neighborhoods populated with communities speaking a host of languages have sprung up. You will regularly hear Chinese spoken in Chinatown, which has the largest Chinese population in America, while in the streets of Brighton Beach in southern Brooklyn you will hear Russian spoken by immigrants from the Soviet Union and Ukraine who settled here in the 1960s.

There are many neighborhoods where you won't hear English spoken at all.

A city-wide census has revealed that the most widely spoken languages vary greatly from one borough to the next. In Manhattan, the vast majority (60 percent) of residents speak English at home, with Spanish (57 percent) the most commonly spoken foreign language, followed by Chinese (13 percent), French (6 percent), and Korean (2 percent). In Brooklyn, about half the people (53 percent) speak English, with fluency in a foreign tongue including Spanish (36 percent), Chinese (15 percent), Russian (12 percent), and Yiddish (7 percent). In the Bronx, where a majority of the population is Hispanic, Spanish (81 percent) is followed by Kru, Igbo, and Yoruba (4 percent), Bengali (2 percent), French (2 percent), and Italian (1 percent).

As one New Yorker in four speaks imperfect English, the City Council adopted a regulation in 2017 that provides its residents with the assistance that may be required for good communication when accessing essential services. The NYC Health Department now offers free or low-cost support to those in need and this Language Access Plan with its volunteer interpreters allows submissions to the City Planning Commission to be made in English, Spanish, Chinese, Russian, Bengali, Haitian Creole, Korean, Arabic, Urdu, French, and Polish.

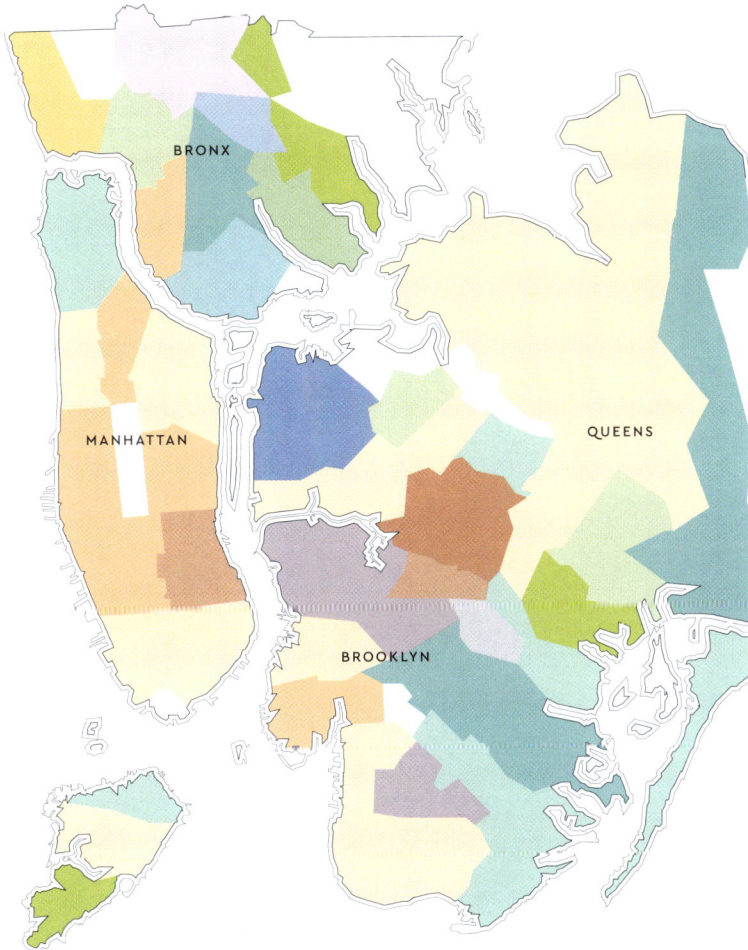

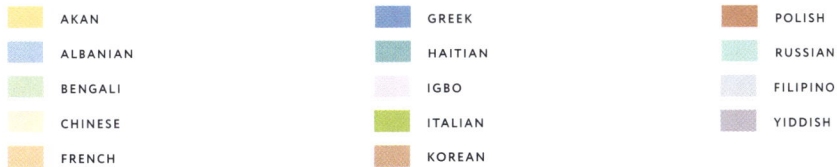

BRONX

MANHATTAN

QUEENS

BROOKLYN

AKAN		GREEK		POLISH	
ALBANIAN		HAITIAN		RUSSIAN	
BENGALI		IGBO		FILIPINO	
CHINESE		ITALIAN		YIDDISH	
FRENCH		KOREAN			

MOTHER TONGUES

More than seven hundred languages have been identified in this metropolis populated with people of highly diverse origins. English is not the norm in some boroughs, with Spanish, Chinese, Russian, and Yiddish some of the most widely spoken languages.

ABOVE

The Lemon Ice King of Corona has been serving Italian-style granita since 1944.

OPPOSITE

The kiosk aims to offer customers a wide variety of flavors.

EXCURSION

THE SOMERSET HOUSE

Designer Alan Eckstein has retained a taste for blending styles from
the years he spent in the fashion world, and The Somerset House,
a gallery of furniture and vintage artwork in Long Island City,
offers an insight into his creative genius.

Alan Eckstein is one of the bold designers currently shaking up the New York design scene. When the COVID-19 pandemic was obliging many professionals to put their activities on hold, he jumped at an offer he received from a real estate developer in the summer of 2020, to set up a vintage design gallery on the first floor of a building in Williamsburg, Brooklyn, at a peppercorn rent (it even came with a glazed garage door). The designer, who has a background in the fashion world, set about collecting rare pieces from a wide range of sources before exhibiting them in this display window sent from heaven. Combining styles, eras, and materials, he juxtaposed Italian, French, and Scandinavian furniture and lighting from the 1950s with Baroque paintings and primitive sculptures from Africa, all arranged in a unique window dressing. Photos of this gallery merrily mixing and matching genres spread like wildfire across Instagram, establishing The Somerset House's reputation in the interior design world.

After this meteoric debut, the young entrepreneur elected to move his gallery to Long Island City in Queens, just round the corner from his family's new loft. "We moved the week our son Luke was born. I wanted to be close to home as I work round the clock. This way, I can quickly scoot back if need be. We really like the neighborhood. We're close to Brooklyn, but the atmosphere is different here, more chilled."

The building the designer had set his heart on at 10-25 48th Avenue was an old karate club. Before he moved in, the walls were covered in graffiti and the glass bricks had been shattered. "We took out the showers, built several walls (using sheetrock, plaster, wood, and glass) to optimize the room layout, relaid the floors, and tore down the ceilings to expose the structural beams. We were trying to create a warm space, bathed in sunlight on nice days, in which every photo taken there would conjure up a different interior." The gallery has an industrial feel, and expert eyes will spot numerous Akari paper lamps designed by Isamu Noguchi and antique wooden screens, of which this aesthete is particularly fond.

Visitors to The Somerset House tend to be interior designers on the hunt for rare pieces for their clients, but this artsy haven is also frequented by collectors and lovers of beautiful objects. Some of these are so taken by the good taste of Alan and his team that they commission the design studio which has grown up out of the gallery to transform their house or apartment. "I love imagining interiors, I would even say it is my favorite thing to so," admits this jack-of-all-trades, who is also in the process of designing a second Somerset House outlet in Los Angeles.

Alan Eckstein burst onto the interior design
scene with designs that go beyond
the traditional rulebook.

ART FIRST

African antiques are mixed in with
elegant furniture and light fittings, mostly
from Europe.

ABOVE

*The mock Tudor houses of Forest Hills Gardens were inspired by garden city
housing in the UK.*

OPPOSITE

A carefully trimmed Japanese maple tree is a bonus on a stroll down Tennis Place.

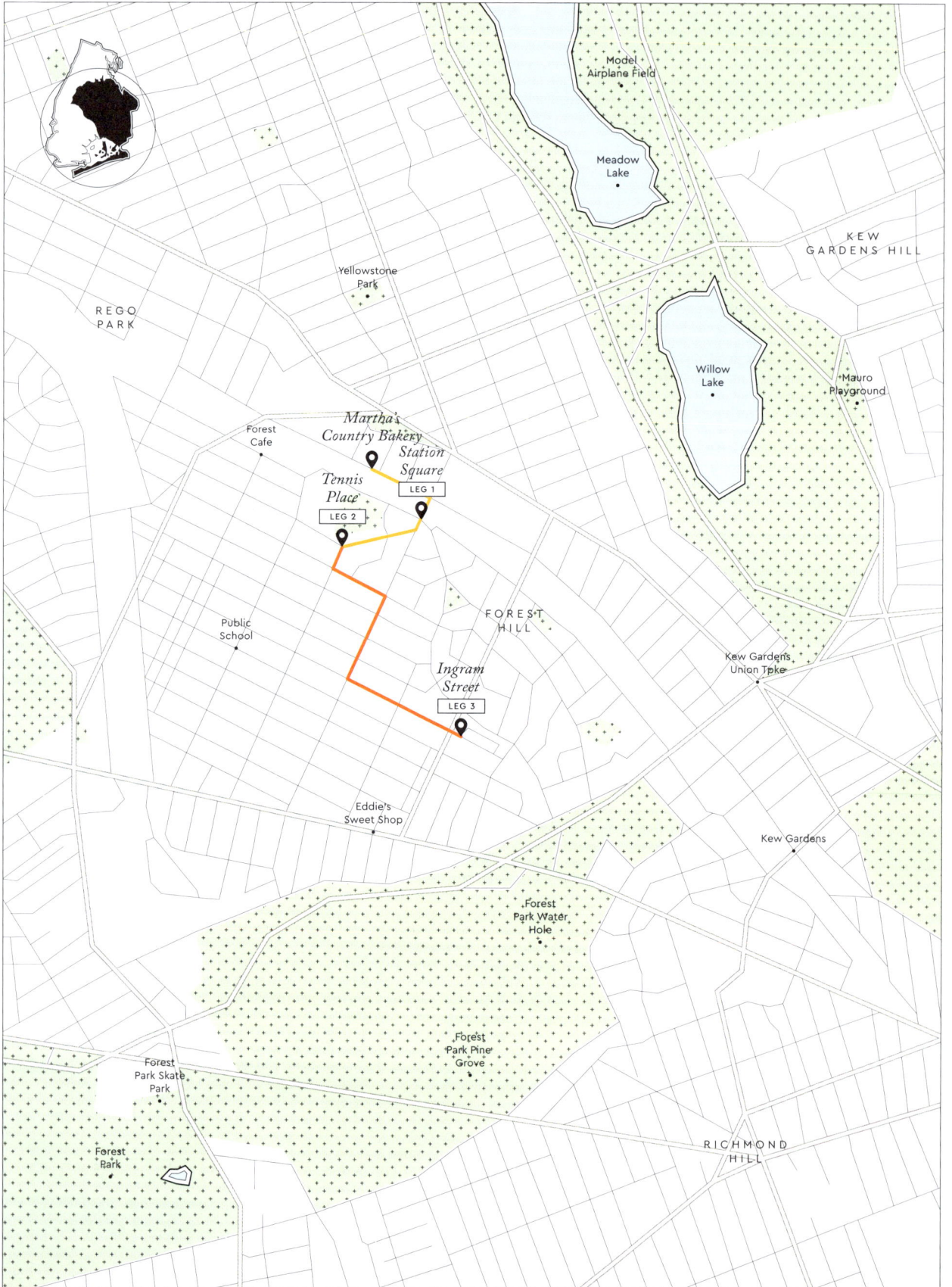

Model
Airplane Field

Meadow
Lake

KEW
GARDENS HILL

Yellowstone
Park

REGO
PARK

Willow
Lake

Mauro
Playground

Forest
Cafe

*Martha's
Country Bakery*

*Station
Square*

LEG 1

*Tennis
Place*

LEG 2

Public
School

FOREST
HILL

Kew Gardens
Union Tpke

*Ingram
Street*

LEG 3

Eddie's
Sweet Shop

Kew Gardens

Forest
Park Water
Hole

Forest Park Skate
Park

Forest
Park Pine
Grove

RICHMOND
HILL

Forest
Park

A SLICE OF ENGLISH LIFE IN FOREST HILLS

Built at the turn of the 20th century, the residential neighborhood of Forest Hills was modeled on UK garden cities. Its cottages and detached houses nestle amongst majestic trees and leafy bowers that form a picturesque backdrop for a delightful walk.

LEG 1 : STATION SQUARE

This odd station, which resembles a fairytale castle, is the gateway to the charming neighborhood of Forest Hills Gardens. The land on which it was laid out was once just a couple of farms surrounded by fields, but the real estate developer who acquired it in 1906 named it after its location on a ridge above the city and its proximity to Forest Park. A charitable organization then bought it to create a new form of housing inspired by the garden city movement then popular in Britain. The houses were intended for middle class families, but wealthier people also had the good fortune to settle in this small private enclave. The project was completed by town planner Grosvenor Atterbury and landscape architect Frederick Law Olmsted (who also notably created Central Park), who banned the use of concrete and shunned a grid layout. Station Square was designed as the heart of the neighborhood, and stores, a hotel,

and apartment buildings rapidly sprang up around it. Austin Street, now the main shopping drag, is also nearby, and at number 70-28 you will find Martha's Country Bakery selling fancy cakes to the crowds of customers often spotted in line on the sidewalk.

LEG 2 : TENNIS PLACE

Head for nearby Tennis Place, a winding lane lined with half-timbered mock Tudor houses and bushes and trees with meticulous topiary. The sports ground next door (after which the area was named) was built to host the US Open championship in what was then the West Side Tennis Club from 1915 to 1977 before the competition was moved to Flushing Meadows-Corona Park. The old complex was also used as a concert venue and big names on the music scene have played here, including Frank Sinatra, the Rolling Stones, Jimi Hendrix, and Bob Dylan.

LEG 3 : INGRAM STREET

Now take a left onto Exeter Street and a right onto Continental Avenue. Continue for four blocks and you will reach Ingram Street, where, at number 20, you will find the Edwardian townhouse on which comic book artist Steve Ditko based the home where Peter Parker, alias Spider-Man, spent his young years with his Uncle Ben and Aunt May. Legend has it that a family named Parker once actually lived here, and the current occupants are said to regularly receive mail from fans addressed to the superhero. In 2025, the house, with its four bedrooms and bathrooms, was put up for sale in 2025 with an asking price of nearly two million US dollars.

BIOGRAPHY

After a degree in journalism and a nascent career in publishing in Brussels, **Muriel Françoise** moved to Stockholm in 2007, where she quickly took an interest in design for European media titles. She has lived in Montreal since 2014, writing for *MilK Magazine*, *MilK Decoration*, *La Presse* and the Quebec and Canada editions of *ELLE Decoration*. She makes use of her stays in New York City to meet those prepared to bare their souls to her.

Thank you to Achille, my beautiful star, Claire and René, who got me going, and my friends, who keep me going. To Sylvie, for following me on this wonderful adventure, to Faris for choosing me, supporting me, and guiding me for this book, and to Franck and Mireille for ensuring the correctness of my words. Thanks finally to Hélène, who mentioned my name to Éditions du Chêne for this project, and to Laurine, who made it possible for me to explore unique talents and places in New York City.

Sylvie Li is a Montreal-based photographer who has worked with a wide variety of editors and titles, including *ELLE Décoration* Québec, *Architectural Digest*, *The Globe and Mail*, *KO Éditions*, and Air Canada. She tries to tell stories and convey emotions through her lens, whether in portraits of artisans, interior design reportage, or culinary art, her favorite subjects.

Thank you to my parents, my sister, and to Auguste for their support as I pursue this profession I love so much. To Muriel, my partner in crime, for her precious advice and the unforgettable memories made in this metropolis, without whom I could not have done this book. Thank you finally to Faris and the Éditions du Chêne team for the entrusting this project to me.

PHOTOGRAPHIC CREDITS

All the photographs in this book are by Sylvie Li, with the exception of: © Alfredo Garcia Saz/Alamy Image bank: 104; © Claudio Schwarz/Unsplash: 75; © David Vives/Unsplash: 44; © Ed Rooney/Alamy Image bank: 45; © Jamison McAndie/Unsplash: 74; © Jon Bilous/Alamy Image bank: 201; © MB_Photo/Alamy Image bank: 137.

The editor has taken every care to secure the rights relating to the various elements within this volume, but should the book contain any aspect infringing upon the rights of third parties, they are invited to contact Éditions du Chêne.

First published in English in 2025
by Rizzoli Universe, a division of
Rizzoli International Publications

Rizzoli International Publications Inc
49 West 27th Street
New York, NY 10001

Rizzoli International Publications UK Ltd
Somerset House, West Wing
Strand, London WC2R 1LA

www.rizzoliusa.com

Originally published in French in 2025 as
Petit Atlas Hédoniste – New York
by © 2025, Éditions du Chêne – Hachette Livre
www.editionsduchene.fr

Copyright © 2025, Éditions du Chêne

For Rizzoli
Publisher: Charles Miers
Associate Publisher: Tina Persaud
Senior Editor: Kristy Richardson

For Éditions du Chêne
Editor-in chief: Emmanuel Le Vallois
Artistic director: Sabine Houplain

ISBN 978-0-7893-4435-9

2025 / 1
Printed in China

The authorized representative in the EU for safety and compliance is Mondadori Libri S.p.A., via Gian Battista Vico 42, Milan, Italy, 0123, www.mondadori.it

Visit us online: Instagram.com/RizzoliBooks
Facebook.com/RizzoliNewYork
Youtube.com/user/RizzoliNY

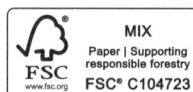

MIX
Paper | Supporting
responsible forestry
FSC
www.fsc.org
FSC® C104723